"Beautifully presented, really easy to read - a compendium of all the best advice from parenting research, based on the authors' real-life experience. I love the Troubleshooting section at the back. It's the book I would've liked when I was a parent myself."
Sue Palmer - Former Headteacher and Author of *Toxic Childhood*

"Offers a fresh perspective that helps parents harmonise their conflicting parenting styles, rather than make them feel guilty for failing to fit into an 'idealised' parenting mould. The practical tools provided allow parents to do away with the good cop/bad cop roles and work better as a team."
Oliver James – Clinical Psychologist and Author of *They F*** You Up*

"A wonderful piece of work. It reads well, it is easy to digest, and it contains useful and practical information for parents. I have used several of the ideas from the book and the mobile app in my parenting courses and they work! This is a welcome addition to the literature on parenting particularly as we do need more made in England publications. I am sure that you have a bestseller with this publication."
Grendon Haines - School psychologist at Harrow school

"Very erudite and strong and one of the best and most pragmatic books on parenting and family life I have read in a long time. I think that the 'Voice of the child' and the practical strategies and solutions will be a boon to most parents."
Stephen Adams-Langley - Senior Clinical Consultant at Place2be.org.uk

"A wonderfully all-round emotionally intelligent book. I loved the format - the voice of the child vs Strict and All heart parent as it helps parents accept responsibility for how their behaviour plays out in their children."
Tanith Carey – Award-winning journalist and author of *Taming the Tiger Parent*

"I thoroughly enjoyed reading Kids don't come with a manual. If you've ever felt that you are the only parent in the world who doesn't seem to be able to parent effectively, this book will give you the reassurance that you're not alone and provide the support needed to keep going.

Carole and Nadim have a refreshingly honest way of communicating the ups and downs of being a parent. The inclusion of the voice of the child so you can appreciate their point of view is genius and really helps give a new perspective.

They remind us that we have a choice in how we parent our children. We can choose whether to pass on the negative patterns learnt in our own childhood, or we can identify those patterns and not pass them on.

There were some tools that I wish I'd known when my children were small, but there are others that I know I can introduce to our family now, even though our four children range from age twelve to nineteen. Carole and Nadim have so much practical experience and knowledge on this subject and it's a relief to know that they have tried out all the tools on their own children."

**Serena Gordon – Actress, Director Hoffman UK
and mother of four**

"Useful, practical and compassionate."
Rowan Somerville – Author of *The Shape of her* and father of two

*"Pertinent and imperative for every parent,
irrespective of the child's behaviour."*
Christine Wallier – Mother of three

"You teach best what you most need to learn".

Richard Bach

KIDS
DON'T COME WITH A
MANUAL

The
Essential Guide to a
Happy Family Life

CAROLE & NADIM SAAD

With KATIE SAMPSON

Best of Parenting Publishing

First published in Great Britain by Best of Parenting Publishing 2015

242 Acklam Road, London, W10 5JJ, United Kingdom

www.bestofparenting.com

A CIP catalogue record of this book is available from the British Library

ISBN: 978-0-9931743-0-8

Co-writer, Katie Sampson

Editor Jacq Burns, www.jacqburns.com

Cover Design by Ian Pamplona and Jennifer Oldenburg

Set in Minion Pro

Printed and bound in Great Britain by Clays Ltd, St Ives plc

To our parents, thank you for all your love, dedication and support

To our daughters Noor, Yasmine and Yara, thank you for helping us grow and become better as parents as well as human beings. You are the light, the magic and the joy of our lives

CONTENTS

Introduction

So many contradicting theories

Parenting is probably the most important job we get to do in life. Yet, although most jobs require training, and there are compulsory exams for almost everything from school to driving a car, most of us arrive at the 'wheel of parenting' with next to no *objective* knowledge as to how to be a parent. Instead we seem to expect that parenting skills will come to us 'naturally' or via the shared wisdom of those around us such as family and friends or, increasingly, parenting books.

There is a bewildering array of parenting 'bibles' and press articles offering advice (and warnings) to today's parents. At one end of the scale are the guides recommending an authoritarian 'tiger parent' approach to bringing up kids and on the other end are much more 'laissez-faire' approaches.

Is the best way to change children's behaviour through punishments, such as 'naughty steps' or withdrawal of privileges? Or should we take the gentler approach, investing lots of time in explaining to our children why we'd prefer them to behave in a more amenable fashion?

Should we reassure our children when they have negative emotions by telling them: "It's ok, I'm here, no need to cry"? Or is it better to toughen them up by telling them in a firmer way: "You shouldn't be crying over this, you're too old for that!"?

Are we supposed to praise our children every time they do something 'right' to help them improve their behaviour? Or is there a danger of turning them into 'praise junkies'?

Should we tell our children that they are 'good' and that they are 'clever' to boost their self-esteem? Or does this actually make them afraid of failure?

Should we make sure that our kids have lots of activities because it increases their IQ and self-esteem? Or does over-scheduling reduce our children's creativity, happiness and independence?

With so many contradictory beliefs clamouring for parent's attention, it's no wonder that we are left feeling even more confused (and sometimes even guilty) about the 'right' way to parent.

A balanced approach to parenting

As a couple with conflicting parenting styles, we were torn between the gentler 'laissez-faire' approach and the more disciplinarian 'tiger parent' philosophy. Yet, what we really wanted was a more *objective* way of parenting together that would be really effective.

So casting the parenting fads to one side, we turned to the research in child psychology, neuroscience and education and devoured hundreds of the world's leading parenting books to find practical, tried and tested evidence.

And we were delighted to discover that there really are clear, straightforward methods for achieving what we call a 'balanced' approach to parenting. In other words that the best way we could achieve a harmonious, joined-up and happy family was through balancing our own parenting styles, while having a good understanding of what motivated our children's behaviour.

So life changing were our discoveries, that we decided to use our backgrounds in child development and parent coaching to convert them into powerful step-by-step tools, and make them available to parents world over.

We decided to write our own parenting 'manual' as we couldn't find any that would cover what we felt parents like us desperately needed, including:

1. A parenting philosophy based on hard evidence and the latest research.

2. A 'balanced' approach that would help us harmonise our different parenting styles, rather than making us feel guilty for failing to fit into an 'idealised' parenting mould.

3. A practical manual with effective step-by-step 'tools', which would empower us to:
   - Deal with everyday parenting challenges without confrontation or anger
   - Help our children to become happy, fulfilled and self-reliant adults
   - Maintain our long-term objective of having a good connection with our children (at all stages of their lives)

Will this book turn you into perfect parents? No! Will it make parenting less stressful and more enjoyable? Certainly!

We are under no illusions about the reality of family life and have no wish to make it 'perfect'. We know that the average family day (aside from any work hassles) includes a large dose of unexpected challenges, a pinch of chaos, a drizzle of fatigue, a dash of arguments between parents, sprinklings of disappointment, despair, fear and frustration, a splash of tears, plenty of cooking and a whole heap of laundry. The fact is that there is no magic wand to make a family life perfect!

However, with a bit more awareness of our children's needs, combined with some simple practical trouble-shooting tools, we can go a long way to making a real difference to our children's, our family's and our own lives. Parenting needn't be so stressful, particularly when there is so much potential for enjoyment, fun, silliness, connection and the sense of reward, achievement and pride that family life can bring.

Applying the tools in this book will not make your children so well behaved that you will never have to 'correct their behaviour' again. Life would be very boring without the delightful unexpectedness that children bring to it. But we do believe that we can help empower you to deal with most situations effectively so that these 'challenges' (including misbehaviours) become opportunities for learning and growing rather than being stressors or negative experiences with our children. Our main goal is that you will learn to use the tools we describe within this book to raise your children to become the happy and confident individuals that they deserve to be: children who are willing and able to stand on their own two feet and meet life's challenges.

You have the choice to be the parent you really want to be

After reading this book, you will be able to choose how you react to difficult situations, helping you to respond calmly and effectively to challenges, rather than with threats, rewards/bribes, anger or punishment.

There may still be times when you will be so 'triggered' by your children's behaviour that you will want to scream, shout or tear your hair out or all three. And for those occasions you will have our 'repairing' tools, which allow you to reconnect with your children while ensuring that each member of the family takes responsibility for their own actions. The saying, 'the better the leader, the better the team' – never has this been so true as within a family!

Our journey towards more balanced enjoyable parenting

Instincts can be misleading

When our first child was born, family and friends said "You'll be great parents, all you have to do is rely on your love and your instincts". We saw no reason to disbelieve this as there is a plethora of press articles that recommends ditching all the 'expert' advice and relying instead on our parental instincts.

Carole also has extensive experience in child development, having trained as a Montessori teacher and successfully run her own nursery. She was used to being asked for advice from other parents who admired her ability to manage their kids. Surely she'd be a 'natural' parent?

We were therefore surprised to find that instead of living our family dream, we were often struggling to agree on how to parent our children together.

Like most parents, we have deeply rooted instincts to love and protect our children. We were convinced that we could rely on these instincts to tell us how best to parent our children. We were therefore shocked to learn that our 'gut reactions' to our children's behaviour actually had little to do with loving 'instincts'.

We discovered that our natural reflexes were much more likely to be emotional reactions to the way we were parented ourselves, what the sociologists call 'inherited parenting style'[1]. So rather than having an innate ability to separate what was 'right' from what was 'wrong' for our children, we were placing our faith in a set of personal beliefs about child raising based on our experience of being 'parented' ourselves.

For instance, our levels of tolerance and reactions to 'mis'behaviour, noise levels, a child's cry and all the many other things that we experience with our children are informed far more by these inherited beliefs than by rational, strategic thinking - however much we might aspire to the latter[2].

On top of this, given that we are all raised differently, these inherited convictions often clash with our partners' beliefs. In our case Carole, had a 'softer' disposition and therefore had 'laissez-faire' and sometimes overprotective inclinations, whereas Nadim had far 'stricter' and more authoritarian reactions.

What made things harder still was that we had such high expectations of our own 'natural' parenting skills. Prior to training as parent coaches we thought, like most couples, that our inherited parenting instincts were useful and objective. This made us more entrenched in our parenting position and lead to endless arguments as it's pretty difficult to argue against an instinct, isn't it?

"You have no idea what kind of parent you are going to be"

Carole: "The moment I had my first child, I finally understood what a friend had said to me: "You have no idea what kind of parent you are going to be". Before becoming a mother, I did not truly understand the effect that emotions, stress and personal history could have on my behaviours and attitude towards my own children. And I have to confess that the result was not always in accordance with my philosophy and expertise. It had been much easier for me to advise and help others than it was to apply my true convictions in my own life."

Nadim: "My reactions resulted from a strict upbringing, which I found myself replicating on my own children - particularly during stressful moments. I believed that Carole was too lenient with the kids and not consistent in setting boundaries. This led me to become even stricter in order to compensate for what I perceived to be her 'failings'. I also felt I was being forced into the role of 'bad cop', which was damaging my connection with my children. I started to blame Carole for creating this situation."

Our disagreements worsened as our family grew. Not only did each child have a very different temperament, but the challenges got greater as our children grew older.

And like many parents, we tended to blame our children's temperament for their misbehaviour, as it was difficult for us to realise and admit the impact that our behaviour was having on theirs.

If it ain't broke why fix it?

We stubbornly held on to our belief that we were, at least individually, 'great' parents. Our belief that we'd 'turned out ok' despite the parenting mistakes of our own parents gave us little incentive to work at changing our own parenting styles. If it ain't broke, we thought, then why fix it?

The turning point came when we realised that for every child who 'turns out ok' despite their parent's 'mistakes', there are others who suffer as a result of their parents' actions in the long-term. We often see in families how some siblings have more vulnerable coping mechanisms than others, and how over-disciplinarian and over-protective parents can leave lasting emotional scars. Shouldn't we try and minimise the chances of us damaging our children we thought?

Increasing our chances of raising happy and confident children

We were also forced to acknowledge that the family harmony we desired was becoming more elusive. Daily disagreements were flaring up, with accusations that one was being too strict and the other too lenient; both of us convinced that our 'parenting style' was the 'right one'. Worse still, we realised that the conflict was affecting our children, as they were showing signs of anxiety when we disagreed. Our children were also starting to 'play us against the other', which would create even more conflict between us.

Having admitted that our family dynamic needed to change, we identified three key goals:

1. To learn to work together rather than opposing one another.

2. To maximise our chances of seeing our three children thrive emotionally, intellectually and physically, and minimise the chances of having them feel inadequate in this fast changing world.

3. To be able to enjoy every stage of our years parenting together and be happy individually and as a family.

Kids don't come with an instruction manual

As most parents are not trained to be parents, we knew we weren't the first people to wish that our children had arrived with an instruction manual, but perhaps one had been written?

To find out what the experts said about what parenting techniques have been proven to work, we consulted the world's most successful parenting methods and the latest research into parenting, including data from child psychologists, neuroscientists and specialists in education.

To our delight, we found logical insights as to what motivated our children's behaviour and our own that were pure and simple common sense. We gained new knowledge and awareness of our parenting styles, that really helped us to be more accepting of one another and to start becoming more effective in our parenting.

The 3 key parenting styles

As we have described above, it is very common for couples to have different attitudes towards parenting. As the old adage says 'opposites attract', which is why one home can have two different, and often clashing, parenting styles.

Extensive academic research has shown that parents typically adopt one of three styles[3].

The Strict parent

The first parenting style is the 'Strict' parent, often referred to in the research as the Authoritarian parent. Like any other parent, the Strict parent wants the best for their child, but he or she tends to believe that unless disobedience or misbehaviour is addressed immediately with strict, 'logical', no-nonsense strategies, their child may become spoilt, rebellious or lacking in the 'right' moral values. Which is why this particular parent's tendency is to try to teach their child a 'lesson' straightaway - often enforced through punishment. Yet, as the research shows[4], this insistence on obedience and control tends to damage the connection between parent and child, and can create long-term resentment and even dependency.

The All-heart parent

The second parenting style is the 'All-heart' parent - often referred to as the 'Permissive' parent - who is more protective, gentle and usually has a more 'lenient' attitude. All-heart parents tend to believe that a 'loving' connection should be maintained between parent and child at all times. For these parents, discipline is usually similar to punishment and to be avoided as much as possible for fear that their child may feel upset and alienated. As a result, an All-heart parent can be prone to giving-in to their child during conflict, and this can sometimes be at the expense of setting clear limits for their child. This lack of boundary setting and what sometimes amounts to 'overprotection' can create a sense of entitlement from the child and it can lead to resentment and dependency towards the parent and others in the long-term[5].

Both of these 'typical' parenting styles tend to 'steal' from their children the opportunity to learn to solve problems by themselves, reducing their ability to become self-disciplined and responsible adults. The All-heart parent disempowers their child by over-protecting them, and the Strict parent disempowers their child because they tend to 'over-control' through the use of 'orders' and discipline.

Our intention is not to 'box' all parents with a definitive label as the reality is that many parents oscillate between these two styles, according to each particular situation and the association that it holds for them. This is particularly true for parents who are the main carer of their children (such as stay-at-home parents or single parents) who may well find themselves 'swinging' between opposing parenting styles - playing both the 'good cop' and 'bad cop' - when they are at loss as to what to do to get their children to 'behave'. However, in moments of stress, the likelihood is that many of us will tend to fall into one of the two categories detailed above.

In the case where parents have opposing styles, the family dynamic becomes more fraught when each partner detects 'failings' in their partner's parenting style and starts 'over compensating', often operating at the other extreme of the parenting scale - being permissive where the other parent is being strict and vice versa. As was happening in our family! And perhaps the ultimate irony is the fact that children often turn this 'schism' between their parents to their 'advantage', using the frequent disagreements as leverage to get what they want. What can then sometimes happen is that attention is away from the child's behaviour and more focused on the clash of parenting styles.

The Balanced parent

The third style of parenting is what we call 'Balanced' - usually called Authoritative in the research[6] - and the one we aspire to. Balanced parents, as the name indicates, have a 'broader' and more balanced view than their more 'extreme' counterparts. They will attempt to take the middle ground in order to give their children good boundaries, while allowing them to develop self-reliance, good self-esteem and a sense of responsibility. As a result, they approve of establishing guidelines and holding their children accountable for their actions. Yet, rather than being punitive, they use empathy, a strong connection with their child, and encourage family discussion and critical thinking as a basis for their authority. In many ways the 'balanced' style reconciles the strengths and limitations of each of the other styles - borrowing the more positive elements while ironing out the negative - to deliver the best possible experience to our children, in the short as well as in the longer term. Children who are empowered by parents who adopt this style tend to score highly in self-esteem and emotional intelligence[7].

Excited as we were to make this important discovery about the benefits of 'balanced' parenting, we realised that achieving this balance was harder than we had first envisaged. What was getting in the way are our inherited parenting styles and the 'gut' reactions that ensue. These tend to be deeply ingrained because of the many years of being parented a particular way ourselves. It therefore wasn't enough to merely be aware of the research to change our parenting 'reflexes', we realised that we needed more practical support.

Working as a team

Our determination to change our parenting dynamic was reinforced by our commitment to our children, and our desire to end the arguing between us.

We stopped trying to alter each other's parenting style to our own version of the 'perfect parent', and instead work together as a team to make up for each other's strengths and weaknesses. Since our 'gut reactions' were often proving counterproductive, we focused instead on finding alternative strategies that would give us the choice to react differently.

So we developed a set of 'step-by-step' tools to allow us to practice and adopt these new parenting skills until they became second nature to us.

The resulting tools blend existing tried and tested parenting methods with the latest research into child psychology, behaviour and neuroscience. When we used our tools on our own family the effect was genuinely life changing – for all of us! Not only did the tools significantly improve our family dynamics - including our bond with our children, but they also saved us a lot of time that we had previously wasted in fruitless power struggles, whining, explaining, shouting, etc.

Finally, we found ourselves able to devote 'quality' time to our children and ourselves, and for the first time family life became truly enjoyable. So life changing were our discoveries that we decided to devote our lives to sharing them with families of all shapes, sizes and nationalities.

Empowering parents

We trained as relationship coaches and incorporated this approach into our parenting courses and seminars. As coaches, we empower parents by helping them to identify both their needs and the needs of their children. With this increased awareness, parents can then choose the tools and techniques that best suit their situation. This structured yet adaptable approach allows parents and carers to be more 'conscious and intentional' in their relationship with their children.

Different perspectives

This parenting guide takes into account the fact that real family life involves many different needs and personalities, which need to be understood before they can be harmonised. Rather than forcing you to follow a regime that you may feel uncomfortable with, we work at synchronising the different perspectives within your family so that you are able to work together as a team. Just like the balanced parent who teaches through guiding, showing and empowering.

To give you this awareness, throughout the book we use two parenting perspectives - the voice of the 'Strict Parent' and the voice of the 'All-heart Parent' - as they learn to harmonise what once seemed irreconcilable differences. These voices belong to us two authors, and relate our own 'before and after' experiences of using the tools on our own children.

We have also added the perspective of a child. Parents have told us that it is really helpful to hear the often neglected yet truly essential part of the equation: what typically goes on in a child's mind during particular situations and why they may be behaving the way they do.

Happy family life

What we - as parenting coaches and parents who have 'been there' - now know, is that a little background knowledge, and some simple and effective strategies, go a long way in making a big difference in the outcome of our children's lives and our family dynamics. Of course, we know that perfection does not exist and that we will make mistakes along the way, mistakes that will provide vital learning tools for all of us. Yet, who wouldn't wish to minimise mistakes that can have negative effects on our children and increase the likelihood of raising happy, fulfilled and confident children up into adulthood?

As the many parents who have used our simple strategies have told us, our tools are not just empowering, but genuinely *family saving*. We dearly hope they will have the same transformative effect on you.

Good luck and happy parenting!

Understanding why our children 'mis'behave

A sense of belonging and significance

To appropriately respond to children's challenging behaviour, we first need to ask what it is that children believe they will accomplish through it. We can really learn something from it. More often than not, the answer will be that they are seeking more attention from us or are trying to gain more control over their lives. What they are ultimately trying to achieve is the primary goal of all human beings, a sense of belonging and significance[8].

For example, children will use 'clingy' or 'whiney' behaviour and often disruptive behaviour, as a quick route to getting more attention from us. And if a child seems to be excessively demanding, despite the fact that we are giving him or her lots of time and attention, it may be a sign that he or she is looking for a different kind of attention (or connection) than the kind being offered.

Lack of control over their lives

When our children feel that they lack control over their lives because they are unable to have a say in what goes on around them, it can make them feel they neither belong or matter. They tend to - unconsciously - prefer receiving 'negative attention' than no attention at all. Hardly surprising then, that children will resort to rebellion and power struggles in order to wrestle back some of this control. And if we react negatively to their provocative behaviour, they will have achieved some control over our reaction and gained our attention, which will encourage them - unconsciously - to do it again. In other words, our reaction can reinforce their behaviour rather than encouraging them to stop it.

Our reactions are key

When we encounter a child who is misbehaving, it is much easier (and normal) to react with anger and frustration, than it is to stop and wonder: what is my child trying to tell me?

The reality is that more often than not, our child is trying to tell us: "I am a child and I just want to belong but I don't know how".

As parents, we need to react to the child's belief behind the behaviour, rather than the behaviour itself. Of course, this is more time consuming and requires more skill from us as parents in the short term. However, in the long run, it prevents a lot of issues from occurring and significantly improves our relationship with our child.

Unfortunately, as we explain in greater detail within the Toolbox section, some of our typical negative reactions to misbehaviour (for e.g. punishment and anger) can be counterproductive in the long run. Rather than building a true, loving and nurturing connection between parent and child, the negativity expressed when anger and punishment are used only makes the situation worse. For the more angry we become, the more likely a child is to look for our love through the only means they know, i.e. demanding or 'bad' behaviour, which leads to a vicious cycle of more anger from us.

And in continuing this cycle of negative behaviour and responses, the child achieves the exact opposite of what they really want. Rather than gaining a connection with their parent, the child achieves only disconnection, the negative attention they receive from their parent only increasing their sense of not being 'important' enough. When children become used to this pattern, they may begin displaying signs that they are 'giving up' on a lot of things because of a lack of confidence in themselves[9]. Alternatively, they may start misbehaving to the point where they seem to want to take revenge on something[10] because they feel hurt and want to hurt back. And this can get worse as they grow older if the child's 'deeper' needs are not met.

Parents encountering such reactions in their child will often feel a sense of hopelessness, disappointment or disbelief at the situation, which can in turn cause another cycle of despair. But the good news is that once empowered with positive tools designed to fix the situation and reconnect with their children, parents find that they are soon able to turn the situation around to build a truly positive connection with their child.

Love and Connection

Our connection and emotional bond with our children should be the base of our influence - rather than the use of power - because it is this strong connection with us, and their willingness to keep this bond, that motivates them to behave 'appropriately'[11]. It can be difficult to accept and admit that despite all the love we have for our children, we may be exacerbating their 'mis'behaviour through our own reactions.

Once we realise how much more useful it is to look at children's 'mis'behaviour as a call for attention and more control, we can use much more empathic and effective tools that break the cycle of negative behaviour by addressing our children's profound needs. To help you put yourself 'in the shoes' of your child, we have included the perspective of a child. In each particular situation, this hypothetical child's point of view helps us better understand some of the typical motivations behind children's 'mis'behaviour as they - rather than we - experience it.

Getting the most out of this book

We have designed this book as a manual with a set of 'tools'. What we call 'tools' are practical and effective parenting techniques and strategies, which are easy to apply thanks to a 'step-by-step' approach.

These tools are designed to support parents through the immediate challenges of everyday parenting, while also meeting their long-term goal to raise children to become happy, confident and responsible adults. They have been adapted from the world's most effective parenting methods and have been tried and tested by hundreds of thousands of parents to great effect.

You may already be familiar with some of these strategies and you may be already using some of them, as most of them are based on common sense and basic psychology. Yet, we hope that reading them in this new context will bring you more awareness of why they work, and will allow you to be both more effective and consistent in the application of these tools, as this is what makes them most successful.

Each of the tools shouldn't take more than ten minutes to read and can be used independently from the others. The beauty of this is that even if you were to read and apply just one tool alone, in isolation, you would be very likely to experience a significant and positive difference in the way your children respond to you (and maybe even your partner). Yet when used as a whole, these tools are designed to bring about the fullest possible transformation to your family life.

Prevention is always better than cure

The first five chapters of this book focus on 'Preventive' tools. These strategies are aimed at giving every parent fundamental parenting skills to enable you to address your children's basic needs. We have deliberately placed these chapters before the 'How to deal with misbehaviour' chapter because we want to encourage you to first focus on using our 'pre-emptive tools', those techniques that avoid the 'mis'behaviour from occurring in the first place.

Indeed, although each child is unique with their own temperament, experiences and set of reactions, most children have similar basic needs. Once we can meet these needs effectively, we find that the majority of behavioural challenges will fade or even disappear. These pre-emptive tools help create a stronger connection with our children and build on their self-esteem, helping to establish a family environment where children no longer feel the need to misbehave.

Our final two chapters are dedicated to dealing effectively with all types of 'mis'behaviours and making our children self-responsible and self-disciplined. Our tools help in both the short and the long-term; in other words, they are designed to provide both immediate solutions for specific problems and to prevent them from occurring again in the future.

Trouble-shooting section

In the final section of this book, you will find our trouble-shooting guide, which shows how our tools can be used to address specific challenging behaviours. Whether you're stuck on how to cope with your toddler's tantrum, are trying to manage a defiant 'tweenager' or find yourself struggling to find a way to build your child's self-esteem, this trouble-shooting section will guide you towards the best tools to fix each particular issue or situation.

Persistence pays off

We hope you'll have many 'light bulb' moments when reading these tools and that they'll bring you the high levels of success that so many have already reported. Remember that some problems may be more persistent than others, and that some of these techniques can take a while to master. Our step-by-step format is designed to ease the transition from your old parenting style in to a more streamlined, effective and 'balanced' approach. Yet it is normal to expect that your old, 'default' style will resurface, particularly when you feel stressed or tired. Old habits, after all, are always the hardest to break so try to be gentle on yourself.

Similarly, don't give up if your child protests shifts in your parenting style, as resistance to change is perfectly normal. Children will often raise objections to 'new' or unfamiliar elements in their life, particularly if they are being asked to behave in a different way. So hold your nerve and remember the long-term benefits of each tool; you will be amazed how children can dramatically change their attitude once they begin to experience the benefits of a more harmonious family life.

One step at a time

Finally, being mindful of each child's individuality, some tools will be more effective than others for you, your child and your partner. So rather than trying to master all our tools in one go, pick one or two at a time, follow the step-by-step guides methodically and gradually incorporate each new method into your interaction with your child. Once you have become familiar with the tools and can see them taking effect, you may wish to tweak them according to your own needs and your individual parenting style.

Personalised parenting programme

Many parents have asked us for some suggestions as to how to make the best use of their time to bring about the most positive changes to their family dynamic.

Given the differences in parenting styles and children's temperaments - even within the same family, we wouldn't advise having a 'one-size-fits-all' approach to Parenting. This is why we have included the voices of the Strict Parent and the All-heart parent across the book, demonstrating how every parent can have a very different perspective on a given issue.

To take this personalisation one step further and to fully support you on your parenting journey, we have also devised tailored strategies, which will enable you to use our Parenting Toolbox to maximum effect, according to your parenting style and the amount of time that you can dedicate to this. These programmes are particularly useful for time-poor parents, or carers who feel that they would benefit from a plan structured around their parenting style and their own time-specific needs.

Whether you are a Mum or a Dad, we help you determine your 'default' Parenting Style and we offer programmes for the full-time working parent, part-time working parent, stay-at-home parent, single parents and for carers/nannies. We also offer to send you notifications to remind you of the tools that you're practising, with additional tips of how you can achieve better results depending on your specific situation.

You can register on our website to have access to these parenting programmes on www.bestofparenting.com/ppp and you can also download our Best of Parenting app*.

*The Best of Parenting trouble-shooting app is already available on the Apple App Store and on the Google Play store. To download it, just search for 'Best of Parenting'.

YOUR PARENTING
TOOLBOX

Coming up in
Chapter 1:

- What a child may be thinking
- Tool No 1: Teamwork
- Tool No 2: Limited Choices
- Tool No 3: Asking Questions
- Tool No 4: Positive Redirection
- Tool No 5: 'I' Statements
- Tool No 6: Diffusing Whining and Arguing
- Tool No 7: Planning Ahead
- Tool No 8: Creating Routines
- Summary of 'How to prevent power struggles and other issues'

Chapter 1: How to prevent power struggles and other issues

One of the key findings of our research was the realisation that parenting is often done 'reactively' rather than strategically or intentionally.

As parents, we need to make many demands of our children on a daily basis. Yet, our commands often breed opposition because it can make our children feel that they have no control over their lives. Typical reactions to a parent's order are therefore a defiant "No!", a tantrum or simply a downright refusal to listen, reactions which will usually lead to a power struggle. Power struggles are a waste of our valuable time with our children. Worse still, these conflicts tend to undermine our connection with our children as they lead to arguments, temper flare-ups and resentment.

As parents, we enter into a power struggle often without realising it, only to find ourselves involved in a battle of wills, which can only be 'resolved' when a winner or loser has been declared . Often, the more desperate a parent becomes to get a child to comply, the more resistant the child grows. And if we do eventually get our way, the victory may well be a false one because when children are forced to do something they don't want to do, they usually focus more on their anger towards their parent rather than being open to learn a lesson. And if it is the parent who 'loses' the struggle and gives in to their child's demand, their child will walk away with the mistaken belief that such battles are a way to get what one wants in life. In other words, there are no real winners in a power struggle between parent and child; there are only losers.

One of the most important ways to make family life more enjoyable and less stressful is to pre-empt and prevent these types of situations from occurring in the first place, by being more 'conscious' and 'strategic' in our approach to parenting.

The solution lies in recognising that 'it takes two to tango'. As with all forms of communication, a power struggle can only exist when both parties are involved in trying to wrestle control from the other. Children will soon give up trying to enter into a power struggle if they discover that their parents are not prepared to enter into the argument with them.

When we are aware of our 'inherited' parenting style and how it can feed power struggles with our children, we are better able to avoid them from happening in the first place.

The Voice of the 'Strict' parent: "For a more authoritarian parent like me, it seems inconceivable to lose a power struggle because such defeat means a permanent undermining of parental authority. I now realise that trying to win these battles 'at all costs' negatively affected my connection with my children in the short-term, and was likely to undermine their self-esteem in the long-term. How much better it turned out to be to prevent power struggles from happening in the first place."

The Voice of the 'All-heart' parent: "A more overprotective parent like me wants to keep the connection between me and my child at all costs, for to lose it would be tantamount to hurting my child. Consequently, if my children started to cry, despair or plead with me and I feared disappointing them, I would often just 'give in' to their demands. I came to realise that by giving in, I was feeding some of their negative behaviours as they were learning that they can 'get their way' if they plead enough. Now I force myself to stick to my guns and use the tools in this chapter to prevent the power struggles from occurring."

In this first chapter, you will find highly effective tools that work on preventing power struggles by meeting both our own needs and those of our children.

What a child may be thinking

I feel like all I hear from my parents is "Do this! Do that!", "No, not like that", which often makes me feel like I can't do anything right. My parents boss me about the whole time and it makes me feel like I don't matter and that whatever I have to say is not important, because Mum and Dad always know better. So sometimes, just to get my parents' attention, I will refuse to do as I'm told, or shout "NO!", or do something I know that I shouldn't be doing.

I also find that arguing works because if I argue enough with my Mum, she usually gives in and lets me do what I want to do. However, when I start arguing with my Dad, he gets pretty mad at me. As I am scared of his reaction, I try not to argue with him. But if I do and he reacts badly, I run to my mum and she usually protects me and tells my dad to leave me alone.

Tool No 1: Teamwork

Use for: Creating more harmony in your couple and family, encouraging family cohesion, improving communication and cooperation, teaching responsibility, developing empathy, managing family outings and domestic life.

Although this book is intended for every family situation, including carers and for single parents (and was co-written by a single parent), there is usually a co-parent or co-carer involved in raising your children. And with that comes challenges.

Have you ever had the experience of being managed by two separate managers, both of whom give you different - or even conflicting - directions, messages and objectives? If you have, then you will recognise the confusion children feel as to which instruction they should be following and why. This 'double manager' situation is one that children often themselves in, and one that becomes even harder for them to follow if both of their parents have conflicting parenting styles. Fortunately,,,,,,,,,,,, there are relatively easy ways to adapt our parenting styles so that they positively complement one another, to the benefit of our children.

As parents, partners or carers, it's almost impossible to agree on every aspect of parenting. Our attitude towards our children and family is formed as much by our individual characters and temperaments as it is the result of our past experiences, including how we were parented ourselves. Our levels of tolerance to 'mis'behaviour, noise levels, a child's cry and all the many other things that we will experience with our children are informed far more by our 'reflexes' than by rational, strategic thinking - however much we might aspire to the latter.

Given these differences, it's not surprising that we can disagree with our co-parent as to how to deal with our children. But arguing about how to deal with our children does far more damage than having different parental approaches[12]. Indeed, disagreeing about parenting issues in front of children can create anxiety, as they can feel responsible for these conflicts.

Ironically, it can also take our focus away from dealing with 'mis'behaviour as we wrestle over how to deal with it.

Our partner most probably loves our child as much as we do and he/she is most likely doing what he/she thinks is best for them. We therefore, need to take a tolerant approach towards our partner's parenting skills, and try to manage our differences without resorting to blame, 'guilt trips' or other forms of negative judgment.

The reality is that once we have adopted a tolerant, rather than intransigent, attitude to our co-parent we are likely to discover that their parenting style is far more able to complement our own than we once believed. And having entered into a new spirit of understanding, we are far more likely to work as a fully functioning and effective team. Being aware of the strengths and weaknesses of each parenting style means avoiding the good cop/bad cop stereotypes which children can so easily exploit.

It is also important to have realistic expectations of ourselves, our children and our partner in order that we don't chase the fantasy of becoming the 'perfect parent'. And believe us, as parenting experts and parents ourselves, we know just how easy it is to fall into the trap of 'perfectionism'.

In order to become a better team, we need to learn to resist the impulse to intervene when we don't agree with the way our partner is reacting to a situation, even if we're just trying to be supportive. The fact is that when we interfere with our co-partner's parenting, we are sending the following messages to our child: "Your mother/father is not doing a good job so I'll have to do it". While the message to our partner can be interpreted as: "Honey, since you don't have the necessary parenting skills, I'll take care of this."

The best way to help under these sorts of circumstances is to step back (leave the room if needed), and allow your partner to prove that he or she has what it takes to handle the situation without you coming to the rescue.

One of the key objectives of this book and the voices of the 'Strict' and the 'All-heart' parent that accompany each tool is to help partners find more 'alignment' and consistency in their parenting. This is why our tools are designed to suit all personality types, regardless of existing parenting styles.

Why this works:

Parenting is the ultimate 'teamwork' and requires a lot of tolerance, particularly if both parents are equally involved. Conflict among parents can create anxiety in children and they will tend to take advantage of the 'rifts', which will in turn create even more conflict between parents. It is therefore important to show a 'united front' even when parents have different parenting styles. Consistency (in one's own parenting style) also helps children have a clearer understanding of what is expected of them.

How to use Teamwork:

- Agree with your partner (or 'discuss' it with yourself if you are a single parent) what your 'core values' are (e.g. manners, tidiness, etc.). Then iron out what you each consider to be acceptable and unacceptable behaviour, which will enable you to set rules that are clear and accepted by everyone in your household (see **Setting Rules**).
- Agree that so long as you are both maintaining these shared values and respecting your child (applying the tools in this 'Toolbox' should help you do this), you will both allow each other room for expressing your different parenting styles.
- Divide tasks: if you tend to have tensions when you are with the kids together at certain times (for e.g. in the morning or at bath-time, etc.), reduce friction by 'dividing territories' and agreeing on the tasks that you will each do and stick to the plan.
- Don't try to 'compensate' your spouse's parenting style. For example, if you have a tendency to be a 'Strict' parent (the 'bad cop') and you feel your spouse is being too lenient with your children (being the 'good cop'), do not become more strict to compensate for this and vice versa.

- Try and be consistent in the application of the tools and whatever strategy you and your partner have agreed on. Consistency is difficult because it's only human to have moments where we just want to relax and not think too much about what we're doing. However, it is very important to send a 'clear' message to your kids, so that they know where the boundaries are and don't get confused by mixed messages. See tool **Being Consistent**.

- Do not take sides with your kids or sabotage your partner's actions; don't allow your kids to 'manipulate you' into conflict with your partner. If for example your child says: "But Dad lets me do that!" (as most kids will do!), you can answer "He may do, but I'm the one responsible for looking after you right now."

- When you disagree with your partner's reaction to your children misbehaving, stop yourself from saying so in front of the children. Remind yourself that there is no such thing as a 'perfect parent' and be realistic about your expectations. If you feel that you partner is starting to get 'triggered' (i.e. losing his or her temper) and you feel that there is a better way to handle the situation, you could ask your spouse: "Can I help?" - but if the answer is "No", you need to respect this.

- If you find it too difficult not to intervene, it's often better to leave the room than allow the 'disagreement to mount' as children will sense this.

- You can then choose a moment later on when the kids are not around to discuss how things could have been handled differently. This Toolbox will give you lots of ideas on how to handle all kinds of situations in a more effective way.

- Model conflict resolution: if you start a discussion or even an argument with your spouse in front of the children, you need to work on finding an amicable resolution in their presence so that they learn 'how to do conflict' rather than fear it. If children do not see the resolution they can be left with a sense of anxiety of what has happened.

NB: If your children often see you and your partner arguing about them, including how to parent them (despite all your efforts in using the step-by-step detailed above), make sure that you let them know that they're not responsible for these arguments. Leaving our children to work out what is going on can create anxiety and lead them to start blaming themselves. This becomes particularly important if the conflict leads to a divorce or separation. Caught between their allegiance to both parents, children can easily believe that they have been the cause of your break up, a wound that they may well carry for life. And of course, if you do find that you and your partner, or ex-partner cannot reconcile your differences we would recommend seeking the help of a couple therapist or counsellor.

The voice of the Strict parent:

When my partner intervenes while I am dealing with our children's misbehaviour, or when I feel judged negatively by her, it irritates me as I feel that she is undermining my authority. Particularly because I make a huge effort to be respectful and not fall back into my 'old ways', so I feel that she's not acknowledging this effort. Conversely, when I see my partner being too 'lenient' and not sticking to the 'limits' that we agreed on (for example, when I feel that the kids are getting away with something that it unacceptable), I find it difficult not to get involved.

However, having seen so much evidence that it's much better not to intervene (as well as experiencing this first hand!), I now leave the room if I feel that I am likely to try to interfere. With my increased awareness of the 'weaknesses' of my parenting style, I even sometimes manage to 'hand over' to my partner to let her deal with a situation if I feel that I'm 'triggered' and I am about to react in an unproductive way.

The voice of the All-heart parent:

Although I have learned to accept that my partner has a different parenting style to mine, I still have great difficulty in seeing him being too controlling, strict, or sometimes rather aggressive (to my eyes) with our children. It's therefore really hard for me not to intervene. When I feel that there are more effective (and more respectful) ways to deal with a situation I now ask him: "Can I help?". And if his answer is "No", I (usually) let him deal with it on his own. I then talk about it with him calmly at a later time, focusing on trying to find a way of dealing with similar situations in the future that we can both agree on. Often, the issue is that he believes that I'm not consistent enough in imposing 'limits' on our children, which means he feels the need to play 'bad cop'. Fortunately, our Toolbox has enabled us to find lots of common ground between us, resulting in much-improved teamwork. The children certainly feel it and they even shared this with us during our family meetings!

Tool No 2: Limited Choices

> **Use for:** *Replacing orders/commands, preventing power struggles, making children feel significant, building self-esteem and responsibility, shopping struggles, morning issues, bedtimes and mealtimes.*

When we order people to do things (be they a toddler, a teenager, a partner or friend) with statements such as "Do this! Do that! We're leaving now!" etc. we rob them of the chance to have any control over the situation. Not surprisingly, their reaction is often negative including protests, power struggles or even anger turned inwards in the form of resentment.

Would you be surprised to hear that on average, parents give 34 commands every hour? And in families where children are more challenging, this can be as many as 80 commands per hour[13]!

We can sidestep this by 'sharing the control' with our children. Offering children limited choices allows them to feel empowered and pro-active in the way they live their life. The key rule to empowering through choice is to make sure that the choices are limited, that they suit us, that they are offered *before* a power struggle and that they are given as often as possible.

Giving Limited Choices is also crucial for teaching a child early on, how and why they can make effective decisions for themselves and others. And as children grow older and are able to make more rational decisions you may wish to increase the number of choices you offer (although three choices usually suffice), until the choice is finally left open to them. But choose your 'free reign' options carefully, for retracting them is rarely constructive.

Why this works?

Children, like all human beings, have a need for control and autonomy. The need to assert one's own identity increases around the age of two (which helps explain the terrible twos!) and then again around adolescence. When children learn that you are prepared to trust them by giving them some choices, they will be far less resistant to your occasional need to make an 'executive' or 'emergency' decision on their behalf. In other words, provided that they realise that they are allowed to choose for themselves most of the time, they will be less likely to argue with you when you are forced by circumstance to issue an order.

How to use Limited Choices:

1. Give limited choices before your child opposes what you might suggest (i.e. before a power struggle occurs) and give as many choices as possible during a typical day.

2. Ask your child to choose between two options, each of which must suit you.
   - Would you rather do ... or ... ?
     For example: "Would you rather leave the park in five minutes or in ten minutes?", for smaller children "Would you rather eat your potatoes first or your broccoli?"
   - Feel free to do ... or ...
     For example, "Feel free to wear your coat or carry it."
   - A great choice for smaller children is, "Would you like to do this by yourself or shall I help you?"
   - Never use disguised threats or rewards within your choices.
     For example, "Would you rather do this or not watch TV tonight?" is not a choice, but a threat!

3. If your child chooses a third option, ask them: "What were the choices I gave you?" and ask them to choose between yours, rather than their own choice.
   NB: Never use disguised threats or rewards within your choices. For example, "Would you rather do this or not watch TV tonight?" is not a choice, but a threat. If your child doesn't make a choice within a reasonable amount of time, says "No" or keeps asking for another option you must make the choice for your child, while saying, with empathy "Since you haven't made a choice this time I will have to choose for you, but I will be giving

you more choices next time." This usually generates a strong emotional reaction, but it's worth sticking to your guns, for the likelihood is that the next time you give them a choice, your child will make a decision super quick.

If your child is older (six plus) and refuses your choice, you can either use an 'I' statement (see tool '**I' Statements**) or say, "No problem, I will have to do something about this, but not now" and follow this with a Delayed Consequence (see tool **Delayed Consequences**).

The voice of the Strict parent:

I really didn't think this would work. I thought that if I allowed my children to decide things for themselves it would take too long. And since I believed that I was going to be making the best decision on their behalf, what was the point letting them muck it up? My attitude led to inevitable power struggles when my children decided to resist my orders, which I found very frustrating. When I tried Limited Choices, I realised that it is possible to empower children without surrendering control. I must admit that sometimes I had to be quite creative, since it is not always easy to come up with two choices that both suited me and didn't sound like threats.

The voice of the All-heart parent:

I didn't like the way that my partner would bark imperatives at my children, because I am more inclined to give them some freedom to make decisions for themselves. What bothered me more was the conflict that ensued. The problem for me was that my 'open' choices were leading my kids towards either serious indecision, or arguments over why the choice they chose was not possible. So for example, "What do you want to eat for breakfast?" might be met by "Chocolate!", which would then lead to long discussions about why this wasn't a great idea. I also learnt that offering open choices can actually create anxiety in little children because they feel pressured into finding answers. However, the guidance and direction offered by limiting the choices is a life saviour, which is why it is the first tool that we share with parents. It's simple yet so transformative, particularly when used in a systematic way and as often as possible.

Real Life Example:

Michael was a smiley, gentle man and father to Maria, aged six. Having succeeded in encouraging Maria to cooperate with the 'house rules' Michael was keen that the rules remain unbroken. So Michael found himself in deep water when Maria's friend Amanda refused to cooperate at bedtime:

"Girls, it's time to brush your teeth now," Michael said.

"I don't want to," says Amanda.

Michael is taken aback by his daughter's friend's response, but realising that his order may have sounded off-putting he tries to phrase it in a gentler way.

"I'm sure you still want to play, but could you please go brush your teeth now as it's time to go to bed?" Michael asks.

"No, I don't want to!" a defiant Amanda replies to Michael's amazement.

"But Amanda, I promised your mother that you would brush your teeth. All children need to brush their teeth before going to bed, but now you're refusing. I'm sure you don't want to upset me?"

"Oh that could actually be fun to see!" Amanda replies with a grin on her face, clearly wishing to provoke him.

At this point Michael began to feel really conflicted; should he try to enforce his rule or back down and leave Amanda be, allowing his daughter Maria to witness the rules being broken?

Thankfully, his wife (remembering the Limited Choices tool that she'd learnt in the Best of Parenting course!) overhears the argument and quickly intervenes, offering Amanda a choice.

"Hey Amanda, would you like to brush your teeth now or in five minutes?"

To which Amanda answers: "I will brush them in 5 minutes!"

Sure enough, when the five minutes was up Amanda was to be found back at the bathroom sink, a toothbrush raised to her teeth.

As Michael discovered, through his wife's use of Limited Choices, we can easily diffuse a situation through empowering a reluctant or defiant child, simply by asking them to decide between two options, both of which suit us!

Obviously, this might not work in all cases and we would recommend referring to our trouble-shooting section in the second part of this book for more ideas on how to solve similar challenges.

Tool No 3: Asking Questions

Use for: Replacing nagging and reminding, preventing power struggles, allowing your child to think for themselves, establishing a connection between you and your child, fostering self-responsibility, diffusing whining and arguing.

As parents, we tend to repeat ourselves a lot when we order our children around, which amounts to nagging and reminding. The intention of Asking Questions is to replace ordering, nagging or reminding our children to do something with questions. The idea is to put our children into 'thinking mode' by asking them, in an empathic voice, what they think they should do next or what the solution might be to a specific problem.

It is important that we make sure that we are engaging our children's attention; when they have their thinking hats on, they are far less likely to be confrontational. For example, rather than telling them what they're supposed to do, it is better to ask respectfully and without accusation or sarcasm: "What are you supposed to do now?".

Why this works:

Asking questions, instead of using nagging and reminding, encourages children to think about their actions, decisions or intentions and to put them into context. It makes them much more likely to answer and comply, than they would have done were we to have ordered them around. This type of thinking acts as an invaluable blueprint for future decisions. The more children are able to learn to question and then work out their own behaviour, the better equipped they are to be self-disciplined and responsible later in life when we're not around.

How to ask your child questions:

1. Make sure you have explained to your children clearly, what your expectations are, for example using our tool **Setting Rules.**

2. When they forget to do something or make a mistake (and as long as it's not a 'serious' misbehaviour), simply ask them a question:
   - "What are you supposed to do now?" when you feel that your children haven't done something that they should know by now. This is a great replacement for "You forgot to wash your hands again!"
     You can use this before eating, after eating, before going to bed, etc.
   - "Is this how we do things in this house?" if your child has not done something in the manner you had expected them to do it (i.e. the way you had explained it should be done).
   - "What could you do about this?" if your child has done something that they need to correct (for example if they spilled something). This is a much better tactic than just telling them what to do, as they will usually know how to correct their mistake (for e.g. finding the mop and cleaning the mess).
3. If you feel that your child is a bit lost as to what they should be doing and could do with a bit of coaching, you can then ask: "Do you want some ideas as to what you could do?"

The voice of the Strict parent:

I didn't believe in asking my kids many questions, why would I when my role was to be the boss? However, now that I have seen what a powerful effect questions have on my kids, I love using them to encourage my children to think for themselves. And I was all the more delighted to read research, which suggests that encouraging our children into 'thinking mode' (as opposed to 'receiving mode') actually increases their IQ.

The voice of the All-heart parent:

I hate having to nag and endlessly remind, it's draining and ineffectual! And to be honest, I can still hear my mother's voice constantly reminding us of what we needed to do when we were kids, and how annoying it was, especially since we knew what we should be doing. I discovered how much better it is to simply ask my children questions, and see that they actually know the rules and what they are supposed to be doing. It makes them so much more responsible, and me so much more agreeable.

Real Life Example:

Most children don't naturally wash their hands after meals, or for that matter before, and ours are no exception. The way we remind them to carry out this task is by asking them: "What do you do before or after the meal?" Proud of being able to come up with the answer they chorus, "We wash our hands!" and then run off enthusiastically to do so.

Asking for their answer to this question allows them to feel responsible, which is much more productive and 'self-esteem building'. A far better alternative to the blame and nagging that we used in the past.

Tool No 4: Positive Redirection

> **Use for:** *Replacing "No you can't!" and other negative statements, preventing power struggles and tantrums, dealing with a child's demands, diverting a child's attention away from something negative, encouraging positivity, diffusing whining and arguing, shopping struggles.*

'No' is a word best avoided, because of its negative effect on the brain[14]. Also, the fact that parents use it so often with little children means that it loses its effectiveness over time, so it's essential to find alternatives to it. Instead, we can use positive redirection, a way of focusing a child's mind away from the disappointment of a 'No' or a 'Can't' and towards something that is possible and positive. The idea is to 'bond' with your child using a positive statement, and then redirecting their demand to asking for something more suitable.

So even if you're not planning to agree to something your child is asking for, don't simply respond with a 'No'. Try instead to start your answer with a 'Yes', and then follow this with a cheery alternative, choice or suggestion to be offered, either in the present or at a later time. This may sound counterintuitive to some, but it works. So, you could say "Yes you can have a sweet after your supper, but right now why don't you have a carrot?"

You may be asking yourself how you're going to say yes to something they are not getting anytime soon: "Yes, you can have a pony, when you are old enough and rich enough to pay for it yourself".

Why it works:

Saying 'Yes' or a using a positive statement rather than a 'No' (regardless of what follows), both acknowledges our child's particular need at that moment and answers it in a non-confrontational, empathic way. They also feel you have listened to them. As this way of responding allows you to 'connect' with your child, it will significantly reduce the need or opportunity for the 'Yes! No!' power struggles that we can find ourselves in.

How to use Positive Redirection:

- If your child is asking for something that you're not willing to give them:
  1. Begin your answer with a question or with a 'Yes' regardless of whether you intend to grant the request or not
  2. Then you have the choice of:
     i) Asking a question: "What do you think?" or "Is it time to have an ice cream/sweet…?" or;
     You'll probably be surprised by how often your child will be 'reasonable' and realise that it's not the right moment!
     ii) Offering an alternative time. For e.g., "Yes, you can have one after dinner,"
- If your child is doing something that you want them to stop doing:
  1. Use a positive command (also called a 'start' command) expressed firmly, but without raising your voice (see e.g. below).
  2. If possible, suggest an alternative activity or an alternative way of doing things. Examples:
     Instead of "Stop yelling," try instead: "Please speak quietly."
     Instead of: "Stop hurting the dog," try instead: "Gently pet the dog."
     Instead of: "Don't slam the door!" try instead: "Please close the door gently, would you like me to show you how?"
     As psychologists have found, putting a positive spin to these short commands (rather than focusing on the behaviour that we want our children to stop, e.g. "Stop yelling,") is much more effective. It's also worth remembering that some kids will keep repeating the same misguided behaviour, simply because they don't know how else it should be done. It's easy to forget that just as kids don't come with a manual, neither do they come with instructions for how to behave. It is therefore essential to express our expectations clearly and positively.

The voice of the Strict parent:

Prior to training as a parent coach, if someone had told me that one should always try to give a positive response to one's child even when they were making an unreasonable request, I would have shaken my head in disbelief! Yet now I've tested it, I see that I could have avoided so many power struggles, arguments and battle of wills between me and my children, simply by redirecting in a positive, rather than negative way.

The voice of the All-heart parent:

I have always seen the power of positivity and believed in passing this idea onto my kids, but there are, I admit, times when it is hard to come up with a positive statement! Most parents will identify with that sinking feeling of mounting frustration when faced with kid's seemingly relentless demands, many made against all sense of reason. That's why having tips on how to redirect children's queries, thereby diverting them from whining or an emotional meltdown, is very, very helpful.

Tool No 5: 'I' Statements

> **Use for:** *Replacing threats and reminders, preventing power struggles, encouraging our children to do what they are asked, giving feedback, setting rules, establishing values and boundaries, clarifying situations.*

One of the most frustrating aspects to parenting is how often our desire to control what our children will and won't do is thwarted by their refusal to cooperate. So for example, if our request that they tidy their room or brush their teeth falls on deaf or defiant ears, we may feel that we have no choice left but to use punishment, threat or the promise of reward. Yet we soon discover that all these typical tactics are counterproductive, particularly in the long-term. Fortunately there is a far better, healthier solution called the 'I' statement – a statement of a rule, which focuses on the things that *we* can control and which we can therefore enforce 100% of the time. And since an 'I' statement is simply a reminder of a fact, it does not appear confrontational, unlike the negative connotations of an 'order' or threat. So for example, "I read a story to children who have brushed their teeth and have their pyjamas on", is much more effective than "If you don't get your pyjamas on and your teeth brushed there will be no story."

Other examples are that we may not be able to control how much our children eat, but we are able to control what foods are offered to them (at home at least). Similarly, it is in our power to decide whether they can go to the park or not (which may depend on whether they have finished their homework).

Remember, 'I' statements appeal to children by relying on positivity and things that we can control, rather than punishment or threats.

Why this works?

Our communication with our children becomes much more positive and logical when we focus on 'control-ables', rather than un-enforceable empty threats. An 'I' statement allows for more respectful communication between parent and child, and being far less emotionally taxing - as well as far more effective - it makes family life much more enjoyable.

How to use 'I' Statements:

1. Start your statement with an 'I' or 'My' (or 'We' if you are speaking about both parents) followed by a positive sentence. For e.g. "I give dessert to children who have finished their meal," is much more effective than "Finish your plate otherwise you won't have a dessert!" Note the use of the third person 'children', which can sometimes make this more effective, particularly if you have more than one child. Otherwise, your statement can also be - "I'll be happy to give you dessert as soon as you've finished your meal."

2. Make sure that your statement addresses something you can control and enforce. For e.g. "My car leaves in five minutes", (instead of "Hurry up, you have five minutes to get ready for football!").

3. Remember to keep the sentence positive (you are making a statement of fact rather than a threat!). It is very easy to 'slip' back into making threats while still believing we are making an 'I' statement. For e.g. "I take children who have tidied their room to the park", can easily become "I won't take you to the park until you've tidied your room." These two sentences are very similar, but the key difference is that the first statement is far more effective because it focuses on the positive rather than the conditional, and doesn't address the child directly (and can't be taken personally, unlike a threat).

   NB: Make sure that you enforce what you state (for e.g. if you said that your car leaves in five minutes, you really will have to leave in five minutes). Otherwise, your statements will be considered empty threats and won't work the next time around. Persevere, your children may initially try to argue, but will soon learn from experience that you mean what you say, and when faced with an 'I' statement there is no point in their putting up a fight.

Other examples:

- Instead of "If you don't put on your coat you can't go out!" try this "I take children out when they've got their coats on."
- Instead of "I am speaking to you, listen to me!" try this (when your child comes to speak to you after ignoring you): "I listen to children who listen to me."
- Instead of, "Please sit down. We're going to eat now", try this "We will eat as soon as children (or You) are seated."
- Instead of: "I'm not going to play with you until you have finished your homework", try this "I'll be happy to play with you as soon as you have finished your homework."
- Instead of "Stop bothering your brother", try this "You are welcome to stay as long as you are not bothering your brother."
- Instead of "Pay attention", try instead "I'll start again as soon as I know that you are listening to me."
- Instead of "How you dare speak to me like this!" Try this "I listen to people who speak to me respectfully", (often a tricky statement to make as it requires that you keep your cool!).

The voice of the Strict parent:

I used to think that I could control everything my children did, particularly when they were young, but how wrong I was! It took me time to realise that focusing on the things that I can control (for example deciding that a trip to a park can happen once a room has been tidied), allows my children to become both more responsible and responsive in a positive way. Learning to use 'I Statements' has not only prevented many power struggles developing, but it has stopped me issuing empty threats, which would undermine my authority in the long-term.

The voice of the All-heart parent:

One of the reasons I was such a softy as a parent, was because of my own negative experience of having been parented and educated through the constant use of threats and rewards. This was why my partner's authoritarian tendencies grated on me and lead to so much disagreement. So it was refreshing for both of us to find a grown-up, efficient and respectful method of getting our children to do what they need to do without resorting to nagging or threats.

Tool No 6: Diffusing Whining and Arguing[15]

Use with children aged 3+ For children less than three years of age, refer to our recommended solutions for solving Tantrums in the trouble-shooting section.

Use for: Replacing anger, stopping a situation from escalating, addressing and preventing whining and arguing, lessening power struggles, teaching children that they can't always get what they want, improving communication, teaching empathy and cooperation, establishing boundaries.

As explained earlier, children will always do what works for them. If they find that whining, nagging and arguing works as a way of getting what they want (even if only rarely), they will repeat this behaviour to try and get something another time.

One of the keys to make sure children realise that whining, nagging and arguing doesn't work is to avoid becoming angry, frustrated or to 'give in' when faced with these types of behaviours. The most effective way to achieve this is to use empathy and, at the same time, 'emotionally distance' ourselves from the situation (rather than from our child). This enables our children to feel listened to, but sets a clear limit as to what we will, and won't, accept.

As all children are 'energy efficient', they will quickly learn that they won't be able to get what they want if we are consistent (see tool **Being Consistent**) and we do not get angry. In order to do this, the technique suggested here is to choose an 'empathetic one liner', for e.g. 'I heard you,' or 'I know,' (see below for more examples) and then repeat it until your child stops their whining or arguing. When we first employ this technique, it may seem counterproductive, as our children appear to 'protest' against it, particularly if they have been used to getting their way. However, after a while they will adjust to your new approach and accept it. Indeed, this technique enables us to stop many situations from 'spiralling' into full-blown confrontations.

An important reason to neutralise arguing and avoid getting sucked into explaining too much is that we don't want to create 'negotiators'. If we only value the logical mind, we'll get into endless arguments and negotiations with our children, and they will think that if they make a reasonable argument, we should always act according to their wishes.

We do not recommend completely ignoring a child as this can make matters worse (in that they are likely to 'escalate' whatever they were doing). 'Blanking' a child in this way can also cause a 'disconnect', which is exactly what we want to avoid.

Why this works?

It may sound too easy, yet if you use this tool at least two or three times in a row consistently, you'll be surprised by the positive effects it can have on your parenting! This is because when our children hear us repeat our empathic statement (as opposed to a sequence of arguments or 'No's'), they feel heard. Crucially, they also understand that while we have heard what they said, we have no intention of giving into it or arguing over it, so there's no point in their trying to negotiate with or provoke us.

How to Diffuse Whining and Arguing:

1. When your child whines, or starts arguing, or demands something that you are not willing to give, try using **Positive Redirection** first. DO NOT start arguing or negotiating, or going into lengthy explanations as to why you won't be giving in.

2. Reflect back what they have asked for, and explain to the child with a short sentence why you won't be giving in to his or her demands.

   For example, if a child wants an ice cream before dinner (and you're ok with your child eating ice cream), you can say: "I am hearing that you would like an ice cream. Dinner is in half an hour so this is not the right time to eat an ice cream, but you can have one after dinner (or tomorrow, or at the weekend, etc.)."

3. Select an empathic statement like "I know...", or "So sad...", or "I hear you", or "What did I say?" or simply "Ohh..."
4. As your child continues to whine or negotiate about the ice cream, 'distance yourself emotionally' from the situation (and not from your child), and softly repeat your empathetic statement (and make sure that you say it without sarcasm) as many times as needed. This approach allows the child to feel heard and avoids you from being 'triggered' by the situation.
5. Do this without getting angry with your child, and without giving in to his/her demands until the situation subsides. If your child's reactions become unbearable, use the **Energy Drain** or the **Uh Oh and Time-Away** tools.

The voice of the Strict parent:

Before I had this tool, I hoped that my word would be obeyed, so being met instead with whining and arguing was infuriating and, I admit, I often got very angry over small things as a result. This created a lot of disconnection with my children, which meant that they ended up always trying to get these things from my partner, because she was much more likely to give in to their demands. Thankfully, this tool is a perfect antidote to these typical escalations and now they are a thing of the past.

The voice of the All-heart parent:

Unlike my partner, I often found myself giving in to whining and arguing, as I couldn't bear to see a situation escalate into one of confrontation and tears. It was a godsend to learn that I could diffuse potential power struggles without affecting my children, or my relationship with them. Being able to bring a non-aggressive halt to whining and arguing means that I feel more respected by my children and vice versa. And it stops me clashing with my spouse too!

Real Life Example:

Anna confessed to frequently shouting at her five-year-old daughter Sarah, who was a persistent whiner. "Her nagging and pestering me for things just wears me down, and then we end up being drawn into arguments, which end with my getting angry," Anna admitted. We encouraged her to learn and practice the tool of diffusing whining and arguing.

From then on, whenever her daughter began to whine for something, Anna simply repeated her empathic statement "I know", refusing to be drawn into giving her reasons, or arguments as to why she wouldn't be giving into her child's demands. At first, Sarah was furious that her mother would not be drawn into an argument. "Mummy stop talking like that, use your brains!" she shouted. But Anna, having been warned that most children initially become angry when their parents fail to react as usual to their demands, stood her ground. And within two days, having finally realised that she wouldn't be getting what she wanted through pestering, the little girl stopped whining and started asking things in a much more mature voice.

When several days later Sarah's three-year-old brother started whining at his mother, Sarah piped up, "Listen Sam, if you whine at Mummy she won't want to do what you are asking for, so don't waste your energy."

Tool No 7: Planning Ahead

> **Use for:** *Replacing nagging and explaining, avoiding tantrums and power struggles, encouraging independence and responsibility, anticipating stressful situations, reducing separation anxiety, morning issues, bedtimes and mealtimes.*

There are many common problems and power struggles that can be prevented simply by anticipating potential trouble.

One of the easiest ways to reduce issues, particularly with outings such as going to the supermarket or to friends' or relatives' houses, is to create a prior agreement with our child (see step-by-step to doing this below). The agreement can include explaining what your child can expect from the situation. It can also cover why it is that everyone's behaviour, including their own, can help to make the situation an enjoyable and fulfilling event. This is a much more constructive plan than simply telling children that they need to be a 'good girl' or 'good boy', in itself a vague and unhelpful label.

It's also helpful to bear in mind all the things we could try, to guard against future conflict and time wasting. For example, if we have issues with our children in the morning, we could:

- Help them choose their clothes the evening before (ideally asking for their involvement, see tool **Limited Choices**).

- Create a routine with them that guides your child through their usual routine -particularly useful when they are half asleep! (See tool **Creating Routines**).

- Make sure that they get enough sleep. We cannot stress this enough as sleep deprivation can be the cause for a lot of problems. Lack of sleep can cause children to have concentration and behavioural issues both at home and at school. Classic signs include emotional outbursts, inability to listen to reason, and being slow to do things that they usually find relatively straightforward.

Another stitch-in-time consideration is to keep children informed about future events that concern them, so that they know what to expect (for e.g. the arrival of a babysitter, a trip to the dentist, etc.). However, bear in mind that younger children (below the age of three) struggle with the notion of time, and may become anxious about an event if they are told about it more than a few hours before it is due to happen. If they are likely to have difficulty envisioning what is due to take place, a good option is to try to role-play the situation with them.

Finally, a great way to anticipate issues with toddlers is to adapt the environment to your child's age. For example, try to put things at their level (such as their clothes, games, their cups, plates and cutlery, etc.) so that they can have more autonomy earlier and they can learn to do things for themselves (see tool **Family Contribution**).

Why it works:

Many issues can be avoided if we plan ahead and think more 'strategically' about our parenting. Children like to know in advance what is going to happen, and to be 'involved' wherever possible. They are also much more likely to comply with a situation or request if they have agreed to it in advance.

How to plan ahead:

1. Identify the key issues that tend to create a power struggle with your child and that create a lot of negative statements on your behalf.
2. Think of what could be done 'in advance' to improve things next time they happen. If your children are younger, adapt the environment in your home to make it more child friendly so that you can minimise the number of 'No's'.
3. Tell your child what is going to happen, or how things should run smoothly and if needed, create an agreement with your child as to how you will both deal with the situations you are likely to encounter.
    a. For example, before going to the supermarket, agree with your child what the boundaries are and set an agreement

with them about this. Be as specific as possible; include for example, how you would like them to help out and whether they can expect a treat. For more details, see solution to 'Shopping Struggles', in the second section of this book.

b. Once you have set up this agreement, do a 'think through' with them. Ask them: "So what are we going to do at the supermarket?" and if they haven't repeated all of what you've agreed, you can nudge them with a short question "And what is the next step?" This helps them remember the agreement, and makes it easier for them to comply. As with role-play, being able to visualise oneself doing things helps us incorporate it into our long-term memory.

c. Ask your children how they would like to be reminded in the event that they do not follow the agreement. For example, it can be something such as: "What was our agreement?"

d. If your child is older than three you can even decide with them what the logical consequence will be if they end up not following the agreement (for e.g. "If you begin shouting, we will have to leave the supermarket because children shouting upsets the other shoppers").

The voice of the Strict parent:

I tend to be better organised and to pre-plan much more than my partner. However, I hadn't realised the value of drawing on these strengths to anticipate the everyday tricky issues I was encountering with my children. I also grasped how powerful it can be to pre-agree things with my children, as they become much more likely to 'comply' with a plan established together.

The voice of the All-heart parent:

Pre-planning does not come easily to me, because I tend to think in a more intuitive rather than calculating way. But once I learned the importance of predicting my children's reactions, I was able to prepare for them. This in turn gave me the skills to be able to anticipate - and thus avoid - typical issues.

Tool No 8: Creating Routines

> **Use for:** *Replacing reminding and nagging, preventing power struggles, fostering independence and responsibility, mealtimes, bedtimes, morning issues, shopping struggles, homework.*

This tool is linked, and to a certain extent follows on from the tool 'Planning Ahead', so it's a good idea to read Planning Ahead first.

If you're like most families, the morning and bedtimes can be stressful and packed with 'negotiations' and power struggles. Creating Routines is a very useful tool for anticipating these kind of problematic areas, because when we draw up clear steps and schedules for dealing with routines, this list becomes 'the boss', rather than us. Once our child is able to use the strategies within the routine, they are less likely to try to enter into power struggles, saving us hours of nagging, cajoling or other forms of frustration. See the step-by-step approach to creating routines below.

However, bear in mind that whatever routine you build with them, it is normal for kids to want attention in the morning and to therefore take a bit longer to do things. If you face particularly fraught mornings, one of the simplest and most effective recommendations is to wake up 15 minutes earlier, as this extra preparation time can sometimes make all the difference to the level of morning stress.

Why it works:

On the surface, children may like or dislike routines, but underneath they all need a systematic approach to life (particularly children up to the age of five years), as it helps establish and re-affirm their inner order. However, strategic thinking rarely comes naturally to a young mind, so it is likely that your child will need some 'coaching' to help them build these routines. It is so important to equip and empower children from an early age with valuable lessons in anticipating, planning and repeating activities and schedules. All the more so if they are encouraged to develop their self-responsibility by participating in, and even determining, the steps and duration of their schedules. But don't expect your child to be able to keep to a schedule unless they understand exactly what it incorporates, and how long each element within it is likely to take.

How to create routines:

1. Identify the type of recurring issues, which can be broken down into a sequence of tasks.
2. Decide with your children (in a brainstorming session) what the routine or 'steps' are that they need to go through. This is best done during a 'Family Meeting' (see tool **Family Meetings**). For example, the evening ritual might include: bath, brushing teeth, getting into pyjamas, reading story, lights out.
3. Once you have identified these steps make a visual guide to this routine, using a photograph, or if they are able to draw, a picture to illustrate each step.
4. Include the amount of time each of the steps should take, or the time at which the routine needs to end by (as the objective is to be done by an agreed time!) and give your child a timer and/or a clock.
5. With your child's help, arrange the pictures (or drawings) into a sequence on a chart, then peg or glue them on and include the timings underneath.
6. Ask your children how they would like to be reminded, in the event that they find themselves struggling to follow the schedule as agreed. For example, they might want you to ask them: "What does *your* schedule say you should do next?"
7. If you see them initially struggling with these schedules, you can do a 'think through' with them. Ask them: "Can you run me through your evening schedule?" And then as they go through, you can nudge them with a short question "And what is the next step?" This helps them visualise and remember their routine and incorporate it into their long-term memory.

The voice of the Strict parent:

I didn't realise that I needed to coach my children to create routines as I thought that just telling them what their regular routine was would be enough. But once I learnt the skill of 'empowering' my children by encouraging them to participate in the creation of their routines, I discovered how much more efficient my children could be.

The voice of the All-heart parent:

I knew that routines were important for children, but I also liked the idea of being flexible with my kids and letting them do things 'in their own time'. However, when my girls suggested to me that they'd like a list to help them with their morning ritual, (which would help them work out how and when to fulfil their tasks) I was totally sold on the idea! All the more so when I saw how much they enjoyed participating in creating their own schedule! Building routines into everyday life also gave me the skills to be able to teach my children how to be more strategic and organised for themselves.

Real Life Example:

When we moved house, we found that the change in environment caused our daughters to slow down considerably in the morning, creating irritation and delay for the whole family. So we sat the girls down, explained the problem and suggested that we work together on breaking down their routine into the specific tasks that had to be completed, and the time each of these activities took (making beds, getting dressed, brushing hair, etc.)

The funny thing was that when I (Nadim) asked Noor, aged six:

"How long do you think you need to get dressed?"

She replied "Two minutes".

To which I replied "Noor, I'd love this, but do you realise that at the moment it is taking you a full half an hour?!"

She laughed and said "Ok Dad, how about from now on I take ten minutes to get dressed?"

We then agreed that she and her sister would take a photo of each task in the morning routine, and that they would help create their step-by-step guide by choosing the running order. We then put their list and photos together to create a visual list on an A3 piece of paper (timings included), which the girls could use as a reminder. And we also gave them a timer to help with the timing.

The effect was immediate; the combination of allowing the girls to have a say in how they completed their daily routine, while giving them the sense that the list, rather than their parents, had become the boss, worked a treat. From then on, every morning they arrived downstairs on time, ready and willing for breakfast, with a sense of pride in their responsibility.

Summary of 'How to prevent power struggles and other issues'

- Be more 'strategic' in your parenting. Planning is preventing.
- Avoid negatively judging other parents - particularly your own partner - as they love their children too and are trying to look after them as best they can.
- Your partner is very unlikely to change their parenting style, so instead of asking them to behave just like you, focus instead on working on the strengths and weaknesses in each of your styles, in order to make a better parenting team.
- Try not to intervene when your partner is dealing with your kids, even if you disagree with what they're doing as it sends the 'wrong' message to your children and to your partner.
- When conflicts do surface in front of your children, try and resolve these in front of them in the most respectful way and try and 'model' good conflict resolution.
- To reduce power struggles, share the control with your children by offering them **Limited Choices.**
- Encourage your children to think (and solve issues) for themselves by **Asking Questions**.
- Focus on what you *can* control versus what you would *like* to control, by using **'I' Statements** - statements that you can actually 'enforce'.
- Replace commands and orders with **Limited Choices**, **Asking Questions** and **'I' Statements.**
- Reduce the use of 'No' to the minimum by turning negative statements into positive ones.
- Whining, nagging and arguing are bound to happen, what really matters is how we react to them.

- The key to **Diffusing Whining and Arguing** is to be very consistent and empathetic in redirecting their behaviour without 'giving in' to their demands.
- Make agreements with your children before an event, and encourage them to be responsible for their behaviour.
- Reduce constant reminders and nagging by making routines 'the boss' and asking questions instead.

What you should avoid and what you can now choose to do instead:

Avoid:	Replace with:
Intervening when you disagree with the way your partner is dealing with your children	Ask your partner "Can I help", or leave the room
Commands and Reminders	Asking Questions, Limited Choices, 'I' Statements
Asking for things to be done NOW	Give them the option of doing it later and if at all possible, let them finish what they're doing first.
Using "No" too often	Choose your battles and use Positive Redirection
Giving in or getting angry when your child whines and/or argues	Diffuse whining and arguing with an empathetic statement
Reacting immediately to a misbehaviour	Pause, take a deep breath and try and think of a more effective response

Your notes

Coming up in

Chapter 2:

- What a child may be thinking
- Tool No 9: Taking a Step Back
- Tool No 10: One-on-one Time (AKA Special Time)
- Tool No 11: Playing
- Tool No 12: Humour and Joy
- Tool No 13: Rewind and Replay
- Tool No 14: Repairing
- Summary of 'How to (re)connect with your children'

Chapter 2: How to (re) connect with your children

Establishing a strong emotional bond with our child is the best trouble-shooting/preventing tool of all. Indeed, when we focus on building establishing mutual respect and affection with our child, we are in a much better position to ask them to follow the limits we have set for them. Once a child is able to trust their strong emotional connection with their parent, they will naturally want to repair any damage they have caused through their 'mis'behaviour.

The child's goal then becomes that of repairing their relationship with their parent in order to return it to a state of close connectedness.[16]. This emotional bond therefore creates a much more effective base of authority than using threats and punishments.

As parents, we usually have expectations of how our children ought to be or behave. If these expectations are not met, we may express what they may interpret as 'conditional' love. For a child to feel really confident about their parents' love, they need to feel that our love is unconditional, regardless of whether or not their behaviour fits with how we'd like or expect them to behave.

The need to express unconditional love at all times is probably one of the greatest parenting challenges we face, because there are times where our (over)reactions may be misinterpreted by our children. When we express our discontent at our children's 'mis'behaviour with anger or other forms of 'strong' reactions, they can often interpret this disapproval or disappointment as a withdrawal of our love. We need to recognise the extent to which *our* response to our children's 'mis'behaviour determines whether they draw a positive or negative message from the experience. For example, if our own behaviour leads them to understand that they are simply being asked respectfully to accept limits, which have already been agreed, the message will be both positive and constructive, and they will be far less likely to doubt our love. However, if they simply feel reprimanded (and possibly shamed), it is likely that they will interpret our response as a sign of rejection, and therefore a withdrawal of our love.

The best way to show our children our unconditional love is by finding ways to connect with them at a deep level, by making sure we take responsibility for our actions, and by also encouraging our children to take responsibility for theirs. This chapter explains in greater detail how we can work on (re)connecting with our child and find more harmony in our family in the process.

What a child may be thinking

I really don't get it. My parents always tell me that they love me so much, but they often act as if they didn't love me at all and I find this very confusing. Take my Dad, who gets angry quite often - how can he love me if he's screaming at me? I am so frightened by him in these moments that I just want to run away from home.

On the other hand, my Mum says that she loves me as much, and if not more than my siblings, but I'm not sure. As the eldest, I get a lot less of my Mum's attention. My youngest sister is constantly asking for help, so my Mum is always with her and has a lot less time to spend with me than she used to. It's not fair, and I'm sure that she loves my sister more than me! I'm really sad because of this, and sometimes it makes me so mad that I hit my little sister. I actually found this is a great way to get my Mum's attention, even if she's usually very cross with me.

Tool No 9: Taking a Step Back

> **Use for:** *Replacing 'overreactions' with more effective responses, understanding your child and creating a stronger connection, building your child's self-esteem and sense of significance, stopping yourself from being triggered and becoming more self-aware.*

Today's parents are pressurised into obsessing about external factors like which school their child should go to, what grades they manage to achieve or what extra-curricular activities their child should participate in. While these factors are clearly worth considering, spending too much time and energy on them can prevent parents from focusing on their child's needs.

It is only once we allow ourselves the time to tune into our child's unique temperament and become aware of their most basic needs - the need for belonging and significance, autonomy and control, etc. - that we can really begin connecting with them at a deeper level. Having built this connection, we can then use it as the base of our influence 'over' them.

The fact is that there is little direct correlation between academic performance and overall success in life. Our children's happiness, well-being and success is usually determined more by their relationship and connection with us and the world around them - which is at the core of their emotional intelligence - than from their academic achievements.

The first key thing is therefore to better understand your child's individuality by observing them, understanding their temperament and their 'rhythms' and accepting them for who they are.

It is this acceptance that allows us to raise our children without judgement, that makes them feel unconditionally loved, and that gives them the confidence to thrive[17]. Unfortunately, reaching this state of acceptance is much easier said than done because we usually have many expectations of our kids. We all wish the best for our children and feel that it is our role to guide them, to motivate them to do their best and to teach them not to give up when the going gets tough (see tool **Emotional Resilience**).

However, in our enthusiasm that they reach their full potential, we can also run the risk of inadvertently sending them the message that they're 'not good enough', which is detrimental to their self-esteem and future happiness. Some of us have experienced this sense of inadequacy from our parents' treatment of us and may reproduce this behaviour with our children without even realising it.

This 'Take a Step Back' tool and many others in our Toolbox (for e.g. see tool **Acknowledgement and Encouragement**) will allow you to let go of imposing expectations on your child, teaching you instead to focus on meeting your child 'where they are' and fulfilling their needs, which will allow them to thrive.

Your child will give you lots of clues if you observe, observe and observe some more. A parent who observes and becomes more 'sensitive' to their child is more likely to be aware of their child's needs, moods, interests and capabilities.

An obvious example of how a child's rhythm affects their capabilities is in the case of tiredness. The more a young child becomes tired, the harder it is to reason with them, and attempting to do so can even lead to disconnection. This is why knowing how to recognise, anticipate and address their changing energy levels can prevent a lot of problems from occurring (see tool **Planning Ahead**).

The second important consideration is the need to recognise the value in pausing before reacting. Rather than rushing in to expend our valuable energy firefighting, crisis managing or sweeping problems away for our children, we can as conscious parents take a more effective approach, pausing before intervening to evaluate what course of action best benefits our child in the short term as well as the long term.

As Shefali Tsabary, author of *The Conscious Parent* explains[18]: "Each of us is triggered on a daily basis by all kind of things. As parents, we are especially susceptible of being triggered because our children are continually around us and in constant need of us. However, the next time your child triggers a mood in you, instead of reacting out of frustration, sit with your reaction to see what the trigger is about. ...

This doesn't require introspection into the cause of your mood, just the simple awareness that it comes from within your own self and not from the other person's actions, will enable you to suspend your thoughts long enough to shift out of reactivity and craft a response that is more grounded. ... Once you accept your child's state, even when this means their tantrums, with your acceptance, there arises a pause. From this pause emerges an understanding of how to respond, rather than react."

In a nutshell, the ability to pause and identify when you are triggered will give you the choice of responding less 'reactively' and more effectively. And if you are wondering what a more effective reaction might be, it is the purpose of this Toolbox to share many examples of these more effective and 'grounded' responses.

Pausing before intervening also means that we give our children the space and opportunity to try and solve their own problems, rather than look to us to solve everything for them. One of the best examples of this is when parents allow fighting siblings to try and resolve their argument on their own rather than jumping in to referee the moment squabbles erupt (see Trouble-shooting section for specific solutions to Sibling squabbles).

Finally, the third aspect to taking a step back is to give your child the benefit of the doubt. We often assume that we know the motivation behind our child's behaviour (see 'Why our children 'mis'behave' in the Introduction), but these assumptions are often false, being based more upon our own subjective experiences of having been parented ourselves, rather than what our child has seen or felt. This projection of our own feelings can lead us to react negatively and unfairly towards our children, rather than seeing the situation from their point of view.

As parents, it's important for us to not just automatically assume that we will always know the motives behind our children's behaviour. We must learn to give our children 'the benefit of the doubt', for in so doing we are far more likely to discover what their true (and often surprising) intentions were. You will find a great illustration of this point in the story below.

Why this works?

When we parent 'proactively' we are much less likely to get 'triggered' by our children and far more likely to be able to anticipate and prevent daily parenting challenges.

Taking into consideration our child's natural rhythm and individuality, and accepting them for who they are, will increase the chances of a better connection between us, enabling us to better guide them to fulfil their potential.

How to Take a Step Back:

- Follow your child's rhythm and find patterns of behaviour by observing your child at different moments of the day. The knowledge we gain from taking the time to understand our children's patterns of behaviour will allow us to anticipate their reaction and avoid many issues, particularly power struggles, from occurring. For example, when they are younger, it's particularly important to identify when they get tired, when they tend to throw tantrums, when they tend to 'mis'behave.
- Choose specific times to listen to your children with undivided attention (see tools **Active Listening** and **One-on-one Time**) in order to attune to their needs and feelings and give them empathy when needed (see tool **Empathy and Validation**). A trip in the car, playing a game, or cooking together are usually good opportunities to do this.
- Accept your child for who they are and identify their strengths and weaknesses. Instead of focusing on their weaknesses, try and focus instead on their strengths. Don't try and impose your own agenda as this will undoubtedly backfire in the long term.
- Pause before intervening, particularly when you feel triggered. Learning to pause and identify what triggers you will give you the choice to deliver a much more grounded and effective response.
- Give your child the benefit of the doubt. Pausing before reacting is the first step in achieving this.

- Use the 'Mindful Breathing' technique explained below to become less stressed and more 'present', and teach it to your child. This technique has proven to significantly reduce stress and strengthen attention and self-awareness[19].

Mindful Breathing Practice:

This technique has been around for centuries but the award-winning actress and author Goldie Hawn highlighted the benefits for children in her book *10 Mindful Minutes*[20]. The process is simple and can be used by parents and children (from the age of five).

Steps to Mindful Breathing:

1. You can do mindful breathing anywhere, but it's better to start in a room where you can sit comfortably. You can practice this next to your child the first times in order to show them how to do it. They can then do it on their own.

2. Sit down and start breathing deeply and slowly, filling your lungs from the bottom up - i.e. from the belly to the top of your lungs - as this energises your body.

3. Focus your mind on your breath. You can ask your child to put their hands on their bellies to feel it rise and fall as they breathe.

4. Your mind will undoubtedly wander, but you need to try to let go of these thoughts or feelings, and try to always refocus on your breath. Similarly, your child may start to fidget, which is perfectly normal. Just encourage them to bring their attention back each time to their breath and their bellies.

5. After each practice, share with your child what it felt like. Talk about ways that they could use this technique to reduce their anxiety, for eg. if they are nervous about an exam, etc.

6. Try to do this two or three times a day. You can start with just three minutes each time (and just one or two minutes for younger children), and then try and expand this to 5 minutes and then up to ten minutes at a time.

The voice of the Strict parent:

This tool is one of the hardest ones for me to apply because when my children 'act out' and don't obey me, I tend to get triggered, which can lead me to overreact. This is because I seem to be 'hardwired' to assume that they are misbehaving knowingly - an echo of my own experience of being parented - and my reaction therefore is that I need to teach them a lesson. I now realise that it's normal for kids to test the boundaries, and I have a much better understanding as to what motivates their 'mis'behaviour. Despite this, I still have to fight to control my first reflex reaction. Taking a step back and using the techniques described in this tool - particularly pausing before intervening and mindful breathing - have allowed me to respond to my children in a much more appropriate and effective way (most of the time).

The voice of the All-heart parent:

I tend to observe my children and follow their rhythm, but I can still find it hard to be able to take that step back to allow me to be objective about situations. I now know that intervening is detrimental to allowing my children to learn how to solve things on their own. Despite this, there are still situations when, out of an instinct of protection, I still leap in to help - for example when my children start fighting. I have now learnt to take a step back and give them the space and time to solve things by themselves.

Pause for thought:

A man came home from work late, tired and irritated to find his five-year-old son waiting for him at the door.

"Daddy, may I ask you a question?"

"Yes sure, what is it?" replied the man.

"Daddy, how much do you make an hour?"

"That's none of your business, why do you ask such a thing?" the man said angrily.

"I just want to know, please tell me, how much do you make an hour?" pleaded the little boy."

"If you must know, I make £20 an hour."

"Oh," the little boy replied with his head down, looking up, he said,

"Dad, may I please borrow £10?"

The father was furious.

"If the only reason you asked that question is so that you could borrow some money to buy a silly toy or some other nonsense, then you march yourself straight to your room, go to bed and think about why you are being so selfish. I work long hours every day and don't have time for such childish behaviour."

The little boy quietly went to his room and shut the door.

The man sat down and started to get even angrier about his child's behaviour, how dare he use such a question to persuade his father to give him money? But after about an hour or so, the father had calmed down, and started to think he may have been a little hard on his son. His son rarely asked him for money, so maybe there was something he did really need to buy with that £10?

The man went to the little boy's room and opened the door.

"Are you asleep, son?" he asked.

"No Daddy, I'm awake," replied the boy.

"I've been thinking, maybe I was too hard on you earlier," said the man.

"It's been a long day and I took my aggravation out on you. Here's the £10 you asked for."

The little boy sat straight up, smiling. "Oh thank you Daddy!" he yelled.

Then, reaching under his pillow, he pulled out some crumpled up bills.

The man, seeing that the boy already had money started to get angry again. The little boy slowly counted out his money, then looked up at his father.

"Why do you want more money if you already have some?" the father grumbled.

"Because I didn't have enough, but now I do," the little boy replied.

"Daddy, I have £20 now, can I buy an hour of your time? Please come home early tomorrow, I would like to have dinner with you."

Unknown author

Tool No 10: One-on-one Time (AKA Special Time)

> **Use for:** *Creating a stronger connection with your child, building a child's self-esteem and sense of significance, addressing attention-seeking behaviour and misbehaviour, improving communication, cooperation, sibling squabbles.*

To create a strong emotional bond with our child, we need to spend time with them. This has become more difficult nowadays, particularly in families where both parents are working. Often, we cannot increase the time that we spend with our children, and we therefore need to make sure that we make the most of this time spent together.

This is particularly important to keep in mind for Dads, as they generally spend less time with their children than Mums.

One-on-one Time is a key way of building a long lasting connection between us and each of our children, and for 'filling-up their emotional bank account'. One-on-one Time is distinct from ordinary 'ad-hoc' time spent together in that it has to be scheduled and anticipated. And because it is designated one-to-one time, we need to make efforts to keep the rest of the world at bay, including other family members while this special time is taking place. The idea is that special time, far from feeling forced or artificial, delivers what it promises – in other words, it becomes an island of special, focused bonding time between parent and child.

Why it works:

Most (if not all!) of our children's 'mis'behaviours are a call for us to give them significance and connection. And when we give a child some One-on-one Time, it goes a long way to satisfying their basic need for attention, which can significantly reduce their need to confront us or enter into a power struggle. Because One-on-one Time exists as a focused island of time spent between the two of you, it is a period of peace, togetherness and communication, which can be looked forward to throughout the rest of the week. Above all, One-on-one Time allows parent and child to get to know each other in a peaceful and caring fashion.

How to give One-on-one Time:

1. At the beginning of a day or a week, schedule some time that you can dedicate to each of your children individually.
2. For children younger than five, try to schedule at least ten minutes every day. With children older than five, you can do it less regularly, but for longer periods. You should ideally schedule at least 30 minutes once a week.
3. Tell your child at the start of your session, "This is our One-on-one Time together."
4. Offer a choice of two or three activities to do together (all of which appeal to you), and ones that you know your child likes. A chosen activity could be sitting together to read, cook, go for a walk, do a puzzle, play cards etc.…
   NB: We strongly recommend that your activity includes 'playing' (see tool **Playing**), as this is something that we don't usually do enough of with our children. You need to remember to let your child 'lead you' in the game that they chose. And don't get too competitive!
   Try not to associate One-on-one Time with shopping as your child may link it to material gain, which is not the point of your connection.

The voice of the Strict parent:

Having a very full schedule, I neglected to make time for my children individually as well as a group. But once I became aware of how important and life changing One-on-one Time is for a child I schedule it in as regularly as I possibly can, regardless of how busy I am.

The voice of the All-heart parent:

Although I gave as much time as I could to my children, I mistakenly thought that it was important to do special activities together as a family, in order not to create any jealousy between siblings. However, once I realised the benefits of One-on-one Time I put my heart and soul into planning our solo-sessions together with each of my children. And I was also reminded of the importance of scheduling in one-to-one time with my partner too.

Tool No 11: Playing

> *Use for: Enjoying your time with your child, building a child's self-esteem and sense of significance, connecting with and understanding your child, improving communication and cooperation.*

Playing is an essential part of a child's development and a vital aspect of our relationship with them. Playfulness comes naturally to children, yet these days we increasingly organise their time and don't allow them to play as they wish. The evidence suggests that overscheduling our children restricts their opportunity to learn from free play, and so reduced playtime hinders a child's capacity for development. Incidentally, the same applies to adults too.

Play is essential to development because it contributes to the cognitive, physical, social, and emotional well-being of children. And play also offers an ideal opportunity for parents to engage fully with their children.[21]

So, do build in playtime with your kids as a regular and enjoyable event (both as a group and by using **One-on-one Time**). While it is said that boys have pushes of adrenaline around the age of two and need to 'burn off' their energy with lots of activities and outdoor play[22], it is important not to 'box' either gender (as some girls might prefer boy's toys and games and vice versa). Always allow your child to be the individual that they are and then follow their lead (see tool **Taking a Step Back**).

Why it works

Play has been proven to be one of the key ways that children use to learn about the world around them, including important life values. Unstructured play is vitally important in giving young brains a rest and an opportunity to become more inventive[23]. Joining in with our child's play and having fun with them, even if it is just being silly with them, not only helps us to develop a connection with them, but it also enables us to become more relaxed with ourselves.

How to Play:

- Set time aside to play with your child (for e.g. during **One-on-one Time,** or at the end of a **Family Meeting**).
- If your child is playing happily on their own, do not feel that you have to interrupt and participate. They also need to learn to play on their own to develop their autonomy.
- Give your child (limited) choices as to what they want to play. For e.g. "Would you like to play a card game or a ball game?"
- Don't expect too much and give your child time to be playful.
- Follow your child's lead as much as possible - this will allow you to get to know them much better and will give them the added satisfaction of being in the 'driving seat'.
- Try not to criticise, even if you think that things should be done in a different way.
- Acknowledge and encourage your child's ideas and creativity by being attentive and appreciative.
- Avoid being too competitive with your child. If you become too competitive, your child may become resentful when you win. Conversely, don't always make your child the winner by deliberately playing badly yourself. Focus instead on helping them feel good about playing a difficult game by gradually increasing the challenge over time. For example, if you are racing, let them have a head start, which you can reduce as they improve their speed.

  Since many games have winners and losers, they can be a useful training ground for some of life's lessons such as the need to accept that there are winners and losers; the fact that practice often pays off and that games should be played for the fun of it, regardless of who wins and who loses, etc.
- Engage in role-play and make-believe with them, e.g. using puppets, construction toys, dressing up, or just using simple role-play and your environment.

- Encourage your child to develop problem solving skills for themselves during playtime and don't over-assist.
- Use academic coaching to promote your child's learning, for e.g. colour, shapes, numbers, positions, name of objects.
- Remember to laugh a lot and share your feelings of joy with your kids and don't be scared of being silly – it's at least half the fun of having kids!
- Ideas of what to do with your children during playtime:
  o Swap the screen and go back to games, paper and pen.
  o Go outdoors and play with nature.
  o Get crafty – make stuff.
  o Dress Up.
  o Hold a 'family disco' and dance together.
  o Have a sing-along.
  o Make up stories together.
  o Play word games.
  o Cook together.
  o Look at art together.
  o Plan an adventure.

The voice of the Strict parent:

I've always loved to play with my kids - not only do we have fun together, but it also gives me an opportunity to reconnect with them, and to make amends for any outbursts of anger. I did have a tendency to 'over-control' when I played with my children though, and wasn't allowing them enough say in the kind of games they wanted to play. This sometimes ended up in stressful situations, where either my children or I would want to stop playing because we weren't getting 'our way'. Now I am more aware when I start ordering them around, and make sure that I let them have more autonomy and this has really improved our times playing together.

The voice of the All-heart parent:

I used to let my partner do 'playtime' with the kids - particularly as they grew older and they were starting to interact more, as I was the one who spent most of the rest of the day with them. I thought that it was important for them to play with their dad so I didn't participate much, yet I'd always feel a bit jealous about not being able to enjoy myself with them. Nowadays, I make sure that I allow myself to join in when they're having fun with their Dad and this creates some great family moments. More importantly, I also make sure that I incorporate playfulness into other moments I spend with the children.

Tool No 12: Humour and Joy

Use for: *Replacing tension with a 'lighter' reaction, improving communication, standing back from stressful situations, building a connection with your child, expressing empathy.*

It's easy to forget to laugh and to enjoy our time with our children when we are doing our best at keeping 'plates in the air' amidst family life's little dramas.

It is therefore important to make time for joyful moments and to enjoy our time with our children as much as possible at every stage. Indeed, one of the key regrets of most parents when their children leave their home is that they didn't spend enough 'quality time' with their kids when they were small.

Humour is one of a parent's most valuable tools. Laughing at the absurdities of life often enables us to stand back from a situation that's causing us stress and find it a little more manageable. The same can be said for having a good family giggle at something funny that's taken place, whether it's the baby putting his dinner over his head or Dad having a 'crazy' moment when the car won't start.

Learning to laugh at ourselves is a vital self-preservation tool and as long as our children feel that we aren't laughing at them, they will usually join in. Being silly together on a regular basis is also recommended. Family special time spent dancing together, playing games or watching a funny movie is gold dust.

Why it works:

If you want your children to be happy and joyful when they grow up, you need to lead by example. Laughing releases endorphins that can change some of our unhelpful (over)reactions to certain situations. It can also help us to show our children that we are not 'perfect' and that we can laugh at both life and ourselves, which in turn helps us build a better connection with them.

How to use Humour and Joy:

1. Schedule some regular play and fun time as a family or one-on-one time with each of your children individually (see tools **Playing** and **One-on-one Time**).
2. If you feel yourself getting wound up, pause and take a deep breath (breathing is essential as it can help change our biological reaction to things).
3. Ask yourself if this 'battle' is really worth fighting. You can use the **Rewind and Replay** and **Repairing** tools if you have already done something that you regret.
4. Try to stand outside the situation and see yourself and your child in a cartoon or a sitcom and find a funny caption for your situation.
5. Create a little code with your spouse/partner - and potentially even with your children - to remind yourself to see the funnier aspects to a stressful situation (see example in the Voice of the All-heart parent below).
6. Have a good giggle. Try to include your child in the joke, for example pull a funny face, and have a laugh together.
7. Always laugh with your child rather than at them.

The voice of the Strict parent:

I sometimes find it difficult to laugh at myself in front of my children, as I tend to take their education rather 'seriously'. But I have learned to put things into perspective and to lighten up a bit. I now know that I don't have to be in such a hurry to use every occasion with my children as an opportunity to drive an 'essential life lesson' across to them. I now focus far more on 'modelling' rather than 'instructing', which means that the family atmosphere has become much lighter, fun and enjoyable. Throwing some humour into a difficult situation (for example when using the tool **Rewind and Replay**) has a remarkably positive effect on everyone, far more so than my anger ever did!

The voice of the All-heart parent:

I so enjoy having a good laugh with my children; it seems to release all the tension and bring back the love. So, when I am feeling particularly stressed ,I make a conscious effort to remember the funny side of life and bring back the laughter. Creating a little 'code' among us is invaluable. For example, I agreed with my partner that if I find that he is overreacting to a situation, I can use a single word such as "Seriously?!" to remind him that it may be better to laugh at this situation than making a big issue out of it. It doesn't work all the time - as he sometimes feels that I take things that are important to him too lightly - but it has often saved situations from escalating.

Tool No 13: Rewind and Replay

> **Use for:** *Replacing an angry reaction with a much more effective one, preventing a situation from 'escalating', teaching that mistakes are ok, (re) building a connection with your child, improving communication and cooperation, undoing 'damage'.*

This is a great tool for stopping ourselves in our tracks, when we find that we have just said or done something in a way that might negatively affect our relationship with our children.

Strong reactions from us such as getting angry, yelling, etc. will usually put our children in a 'fight or flight' state. Once somebody is in 'fight or flight', they cannot process the information properly. We therefore end up losing a lot of energy in trying to teach our kids a lesson at a time where they cannot learn anything.

Thankfully, if we can catch ourselves early enough, we can change this situation and take our children out from the 'fight or flight' mode into a more positive and responsive state by using Rewind and Replay.

The Rewind and Replay tool allows us to retrace our steps, out loud, to where we lost our temper with our children. Once we have done this we can go back to the beginning of the interaction and then start over again, this time with more respect, humour and empathy. It can help to do a mental run-through of the tools within our toolbox regularly to remind yourself of better alternatives to losing your temper.

In order to make this possible, we have to try and identify our temper 'triggers' (see tool **Taking a Step Back**). While it's totally normal for our children to push our buttons, with a bit of hindsight (i.e. when we're calmer) or with the help of someone else's objective opinion, we may realise that we are overreacting to things that might not seem very important to others (for e.g. the pristine condition of the white sofa or our children's selfish behaviour...).

Many of our triggers, or 'Achilles' Heels', can be traced back to our childhood[24]. This is why we need to be mindful of the fact that our anger might not actually be due to our child's behaviour, but rather to an unresolved issue that it has triggered in us.

The tools in this Toolbox will help you overcome some of these triggers without the need to search through your past for clues.

Why this works:

Rewind and Replay allows you to diffuse a potentially negative emotional situation between you and your child, and then to start over again. Modelling this ability to 'grab the reigns back' from a feeling or reaction that was threatening to take you over, serves as an excellent lesson in regaining self-control and connection. Not only will Rewind and Replay teach your children how to keep their heads, but it can also lend humour to a situation and diffuse any residual anger.

How to Rewind and Replay

1. Identify your triggers and try to recognise the feelings behind them.
2. When you feel you're being triggered and you catch yourself doing or saying something to your children (or indeed to your partner) that you would rather do differently, STOP and say "Rewind" loudly.
3. Pause and take a deep breath (research shows that taking a deep breath helps significantly in reducing the 'unhelpful impulse' created by your being triggered).
4. Then take the situation back to where you went 'off course'.
5. Start over again, this time with more respect, humour and empathy using the tools within this Toolbox.

The voice of the Strict parent:

One of my key discoveries in parenting was that my children go into a 'fight or flight mode' as soon as I get angry and raise my voice. And that they are so overwhelmed by my reaction that they are unable to listen to the lesson I am shouting at them. Learning that shouted words are wasted words (and wasted energy) really motivated me to change my behaviour and tame my temper.

Nonetheless, old habits or reflexes die-hard so there are still occasions when I find myself losing my temper and shouting. Rewind and Replay is my favourite tool because it allows me to correct a mistake (i.e. when I lose my temper), by taking action to stop the situation from spiralling out of control and upsetting my children. Now, when I find myself mid-yell, I manage to stop myself in my tracks, say "Rewind!" and replay the scene in a more respectful way. This diffuses the tense situations and gets us back onto a friendlier footing. It also teaches my children that no one is perfect and that we just need to learn how to manage our emotions.

The voice of the All-heart parent:

Even though I tend to be a more patient parent than my partner, my children are still able to push my buttons, which means that at times they find that their usually gentle Mum can suddenly snap. Obviously, I don't like 'oscillating' in this way, particularly if it means my children see me as unpredictable. So, this tool is invaluable for getting me beyond that sense of feeling guilty for how I'm behaving and blaming myself. I have moved towards accepting that it is human to err occasionally, and good to reconnect.

What amazed me the most is that my six-year-old daughter actually started using this tool herself. One day I was helping her do something and she wasn't happy with the way that I did it so she shouted at me: "Mummy, not like this!" I just looked up in disbelief, and then she said "Rewind!" and replayed the scene, but this time speaking to me in a polite voice. I was speechless and very proud of her ability to recognise her error and take responsibility for her action so fast.

Real Life Example:

After much stress and arguing around nine-year-old Julian's failure to do his homework on time, his father Martin has decided to take a new approach. Rather than venting his frustration over Julian's inability to take responsibility for his own work, Martin sits his son down to discuss the situation. The two agree that Julian will take responsibility for his homework and stay in his room every day to complete his homework before playing on his computer. Martin also agrees that he start using a reasonable tone of voice with his son, rather than shouting at him or resorting to blame and shame.

The plan seems to work until, on entering Julian's room one day Martin sees Julian apparently playing on his iPad rather than working. Martin is so frustrated by what he sees as Julian's refusal to honour their agreement that he forgets his own side of the agreement, and yells at his son at the top of this voice:

"I can't believe that you're playing on the iPad while you said you were going to do your homework!"

Grabbing the iPad from out of his son's hand he continues shouting:

"I'm confiscating this for a month!"

But when Martin sees Julian's face crumple in response to his anger, he suddenly realises that he has gone too far. Fortunately, he recalls a handy tool he learnt on the Best of Parenting course called 'Rewind and Replay' and immediately interrupts his own outburst with a: "Rewind!"

Returning the iPad to his son, he takes a deep breath, steps back to the entrance of the room and begins to replay the scene again in his mind, working out how he can replace his anger with a far more respectful and effective comment. Seeing that his father has calmed down, Julian now feels safe enough to be able to tell his father what's really going on.

"But Dad I am doing my homework, if you take a look at the screen you will see that it shows my maths research, not a game."

The beauty of the Rewind and Replay tool is that it allows us to replace a knee-jerk angry response with a 'soft start', as well as allowing us to make amends for jumping to conclusions without giving our children the benefit of the doubt.

Even if Julian didn't have a good excuse for using the iPad, Martin could have still used Rewind and then applied <u>Logical Consequences</u> with empathy and without anger. This would've made Julian much more likely to honour his agreement the next time around, than had his father punished him in anger.

Tool No 14: Repairing

> **Use for:** *Teaching forgiveness and to show that mistakes are an opportunity for learning, (re)building a connection, undoing 'damage', communication, giving feedback.*

Many of the things we do with our children when we 'lose control', such as yelling, getting angry, shaming with words, using any kind of physical aggression, etc. create a disconnection between our children and ourselves. Losing connection with our children is a sad loss. Not only do our children crave connection, but it is also our connection with them that makes them want to behave well (see 'Understanding why our children misbehave' in our Introduction). So it is essential that we 'repair' the conflict or outburst wherever possible, thereby restoring the connection and removing their fear of being punished.

Children are just learning to be emotionally mature, and it is therefore unrealistic to expect them to instigate making amends (although they sometimes do, particularly if they've been coached to do it). If we try to force them to say sorry when they don't feel sorry, we are merely encouraging them to lie just for the sake of our getting an apology. Far better to first offer the apology ourselves. In other words, if we want our children to say sorry and to mean it, we need to model it by saying sorry first.

We can then each take responsibility for our actions and even discuss what we could do differently the next time around.

Why this works:

Connection with our children, rather than the use of power, should lie at the heart of our influence 'over' our children, because it is what makes them want to behave appropriately. It is therefore essential, that both you and your child are able to address and repair any misunderstandings, outbursts and any kind of conflict before they do any lasting damage. Reparation of this kind acts as a foundation for better levels of trust, communication and connection between you, both now and in the future.

How to Repair:

1. You can apologise to your child straight after an incident if you have lost your temper or done something that you immediately regretted. However, we're talking here about how to 'repair' the relationship beyond this initial apology. This is particularly useful if you are like some 'Strict' parents who find it difficult to apologise when they haven't managed to calm down yet.

2. Sit down with your child once you're both calm (this can be several hours after the incident) and apologise for what happened.

3. Present them with your version of the facts, ideally using an 'I feel' message. e.g. "When you were arguing so much it made me angry."

4. Make sure that you tell your child the things you regret about your own behaviour, and that this is not the best way to react to these things. Often by this point, your child will be apologising themselves, taking responsibility for what they did and hugging you (but don't despair if they don't as this can sometimes take time for them!).

5. Let your child share their view of the event and make them feel that you have understood their point of view by using **Active Listening**. For e.g. "So you felt that I was ignoring you?"

6. (Optional step): you can finish with a **Problem Solving** session to define what you could both do to prevent this from happening again. If you do this, make sure that you are not putting all the responsibility on your child, it is important that you find ideas of what you could do differently as well.

7. (Optional step): Children need to be reminded that their parent's love is unconditional even if we sometimes overreact (and even scare them a bit). From time to time, it's important to remind them that we still love them just as much as we ever did, regardless of the circumstances.

The voice of the Strict parent:

I thought that if I apologised to my children and admitted that I was wrong they would see me as weak and fallible. So instead, I'd usually blame them for making me angry in the first place. I realised that this was a negative form of modelling; not only was it somewhat unfair, but it was also leading my children to start blaming everyone else for their mistakes. Witnessing their parent being able to apologise and admit that they are wrong actually teaches children that no one is perfect, and that we all need to work on tempering our reactions. I now ensure that I 'repair' after every conflict, and I tell my children that I love them no matter what. My belief in this modelling strategy (see tool **Modelling**) was confirmed when my daughter came to me after an argument and told me: "I want you to know that I love you even when you get angry at me."

The voice of the All-heart parent:

I used to apologise a lot if I was unhappy with the way I treated my children, so this wasn't new to me. However, I usually apologised very rapidly after a conflict, and did it in such a way that they were unable to draw much of a lesson from my behaviour and theirs. I now take the time to sit down with my child once the emotions have settled and I go through the whole repairing process. This really ensures that we reconnect fully and that I show them that I am taking responsibility for my own actions.

Real Life Example:

One day at the dinner table when we were eating a meal with five-year-old Noor and her cousins, Noor's table manners were getting out of hand. I, her mother, made several negative comments, but she didn't listen and continued eating so sloppily that I lost my temper and shouted from across the table.

"Noor, I can't believe that you're eating this way! Haven't we taught you how to eat properly?"

The look on Noor's face showed that she felt shamed and hurt at the way I had treated her in front of her cousins, yet she continued to mess about with her food. I tried once more to reason with her, but I realised that telling her off in front of her cousins was clearly not working so I didn't say anything else to her at the time. When I was putting Noor to bed later that night, I told her:

"I am really sorry to have shouted at you during dinner time. When you ate your dinner the way you did (and I raised my eyebrows to the ceiling) and you didn't listen to me, I didn't feel respected and I felt like you had forgotten all your good manners. This made me angry.

Noor had a sad look on her face and I could feel that she understood my feelings.

I then added: "I promise to find a better way to get my message across next time instead of speaking to you like this in front of your friends. What would you like me to tell you so that you remember that it is unacceptable to eat this way?"

When I finished, Noor burst into tears, threw her arms around me and gave me a long hug. She then said: "I'm sorry that I ate like this and didn't listen to you, Mummy. Next time, I would prefer if you could just ask me: "Noor, is this the way we eat in this house?"

From then on, Noor paid a lot more attention to the way that she ate at the table, and a simple question (and sometimes just a look) was usually enough to get her back on the right track.

When you find yourself getting angry, as we all do from time to time, remember the power of repairing the situation later. For when we apologise to our children, they are much more likely to feel connected to us and understand their own responsibilities and the power of forgiveness.

Summary of 'How to (re)connect with your children'

- Your connection and emotional bond with your children should be the base of your authority - rather than the use of 'power' such as threats and punishments.
- Observe your children and accept them for who they are. Having too many expectations of your child can make them feel that they are 'not good enough'.
- Feeling connected to you and experiencing your unconditional love makes your children want to behave 'appropriately'.
- Unconditional love means expressing unconditional empathy for your children (regardless of what they say or do), rather than blaming, shaming or discounting them.
- Pause before intervening, particularly if you feel triggered, as this will give you an opportunity to have a more grounded and effective response.
- Give your children the benefit of the doubt as you can often misjudge their intentions.
- Special One-on-one Time with each child is essential to fill-up their 'emotional bank account'.
- Play more often with your children. Play makes connections stronger and provides great learning opportunities.
- Lighten your children's load. They need 'unstructured' playtime (ideally outdoors and without the use of technology).
- Humour and laughter can brighten many sticky situations.
- Any form of strong reaction on our part puts our children in a 'fight or flight' state, and they cannot learn anything in this state.
- Be aware that you can do things differently and stop any situation from 'escalating' by using **Rewind and Replay**.
- Always **Repair** after a difficult moment to keep the connection strong and to model 'owning one's mistakes'.

Your notes:

Coming up in
Chapter 3:

- What a child may be thinking
- Tool No 15: Modelling (AKA Leading by Example)
- Tool No 16: Taking Good Care of Yourself (AKA Giving Yourself a Break)
- Tool No 17: Being Consistent
- Summary of 'How to be a good role model to you children'

Chapter 3: How to be a good role model to your children

Children spend on average about 18 years in our care, and during this time they are themselves training to become adults and to become parents. This means that a lot of things that we do (or don't do) in their presence will have a strong influence on them, whether we intend it to or not. It is therefore essential, to be more aware of how our own behaviour may influence our children's development, whether it be positively or negatively.

Our attitudes and our approach to life have a significant impact on how our children behave. On our parenting courses, we have seen many parents experience dramatic changes in their family dynamics because they have simply learnt to become more confident and less 'controlling'.

Yet often, these parents will not even be aware of what they have done differently, and are therefore surprised, by what has happened: "I don't feel that I have changed anything, but my child has started behaving much better" is a response we often hear.

A simple explanation is that as soon as a parent feels more confident and more 'in control' of their parenting role, they become more consistent and less prone to having their buttons pushed, which is enough of a shift to change family dynamics for the better.

This chapter explains how to work on being the best role model you can be for your children.

What a child may be thinking

I get anxious when my parents are fighting because I am afraid that they are going to end up divorcing, and I see how difficult this is for my friend Jack whose parents divorced. The fact that I'm the one who is often responsible for starting the argument between them doesn't help.

My parents often ask me to do something that they don't even do themselves, so it's unfair. They often use lots of words that they tell me not to use and I get confused by this. I wonder why they get so wound up and sometimes angry when I swear or speak to them in what they call a 'disrespectful' tone of voice, while they often swear or speak to me rudely. It doesn't seem fair at all! It's actually kind of fun to swear and back talk as it immediately puts my parents in a 'state', and I have some control over them by just saying a few words.

⊗ Tool No 15: Modelling (AKA Leading by Example)

> *Use for: Preventing many issues from occurring, establishing boundaries, dealing with misbehaviour, correcting 'bad' manners, communication, mealtime issues, making children feel significant.*

Have you ever noticed how the more stressed we are the more stressed our children are?

This phenomenon is due to what are called 'Mirror Neurons' - a reaction in the brains of humans, which means that our own reactions and emotions are likely to be influenced by the reactions and emotions of those around us[25]. Knowing that our behaviour has an impact on our children means that we can be more aware of how we react to them and influence them.

In addition to Mirror Neurons, children also experience 'deferred imitation'[26]. This means that although they reproduce the behaviour and actions that they observe, they often don't reproduce them until a later date. The fact is that children spend the better part of 18 years (if not more) training to become adults, and their main teachers in the art of 'adulthood' are their parents. Indeed, it is no wonder that role modelling, or demonstrating through our own speech and actions how we would like our children to behave, is the cornerstone of parenting. Consequently, the first step towards truly effective, nurturing modelling techniques is to be more conscious of what we say and 'how' we say it.

Yet in the hurly burly of everyday life it is so easy to forget, or even be unaware of the impact our own behaviour can have on our children. For example, if we are in the habit of shouting at our kids in order to get them to do things, our children are likely to copy us and shout back at us. Unfortunately, by the time we realise this pattern of mirrored behaviour, it is often rather late in the day, which means that we have to work harder on changing a habit that has become ingrained (see **Effective Communication**).

When we use our own behaviour to show our children that we are invested in doing things that are good for our sense of wellbeing (whether eating healthily, going to work, seeing friends or getting regular exercise), we are teaching them to internalise these values and build them into their own lives. Conversely, the notion of sacrificing everything for the sake of the children, particularly if it involves martyrdom, can lead to problems both for the parent in the short term and for the child in the long term (see tool **Taking good care of yourself**). When children are aware that their existence has 'impaired' their parents' quality of life, they may grow up to feel guilty, resentful, or with a tendency to sacrifice their own happiness in a similar fashion.

How to use Modelling:

- Respect yourself, others and your environment.
- Take good care of yourself by making sure that your needs are also met.
- Remember that when we get stressed, they get stressed, when we get angry, they cannot remain calm (Mirror Neurons). So try to find alternatives to becoming distressed or agitated yourself (see Humour and Rewind and Repairing).
- We need to learn to control our emotions so that they can learn to control theirs
- Model empathy, respect and kindness and you will have kids that are empathetic, respectful and kind. One of the most effective tools to model empathy and diffuse any situation is to give a hug to our children.
- Show them how to do things; if you want young children to do things properly, give them a demonstration, and break any task up into sequences of actions.
- Model Sharing and Gratitude. For example, at the end of each day when you are putting your children to bed, tell them something about your day and show gratitude for something that has happened. You can then ask them to share with you their own 'saddest' and 'happiest time' moment during their day.

- And last but not least, remember to model joy! We all want our children to be happy and for them to experience joyfulness, both in themselves and in others. We sometimes forget that the best way to achieve this is by modelling it ourselves. See tools **Playing** and **Humour and Joy.**

The voice of the strict parent:

When I became a parent it took me years to realise how much my Dad had influenced my own parenting behaviour. It's funny how one forgets how much is learned at one's own parents' knee. The way our parents treat us is absorbed by us from an early age as a model of how people treat each other. Many people who have had a strict, authoritarian parent like myself rebel against such an attitude, either in childhood or later in life. Only once I had dug deeper to understand the negative effect that such strict parenting had had on me as a child, was I able to recognise in my children's faces the same fear and resentment I'd experienced when being shouted at or disrespected by my own parents. And it was at this point that the penny finally dropped, and I recognised that their own tendency to shout or disrespect me was often their mirroring of my behaviour, just as I had mirrored my own father's.

The voice of the All-heart parent:

I knew from having run a nursery school how important it is to lead children by example. Yet when having my own children, I became so absorbed in my love for them that I forgot to stand back from the situation to pay attention to my own key role as a model. Consequently, I fell into 'reflex parenting', reacting to my children and the situations they presented me with, with my heart rather than my head. The love we feel for our own children, including our desire to protect them can so easily lead us to 'over-parent', a trap I fell into the moment I gave birth. Perhaps the hardest lesson an All-heart parent like me has to learn is that of teaching one's own child the art of independence, and that the best way to do this is by modelling this quality through one's own behaviour.

I had to learn to let go, to acknowledge that my children could survive without my tending to their every need or guarding them against any possible disappointment. Once I allowed them to become more pro-active in their own lives, and stopped being dependent on them for my own sense of self-worth, I saw them become much confident.

⊗ Tool No 16: Taking Good Care of Yourself (AKA Giving Yourself a Break)

Use for: Restoring your energy, putting things into perspective, enriching the family through your own happiness, teaching by example.

Why take care of yourself? Because when we take good care of ourselves, we are in a better position to take care of others. It's a lot like that instruction in the airplane safety demonstration, which tells us that we must attend to our own oxygen mask before putting one on a child. Taking good care of ourselves means making sure that we have balance in our lives, are able to find time for ourselves, and can know the limits to our patience.

All of us are prone to falling into common 'parenting traps', or in other words, a habitual way of reacting to a child or a family dynamic that isn't healthy for any of us. Common parenting traps include constantly blaming our children or ourselves for their behaviour, or blaming our co-parent for their behaviour.

We need to free ourselves from the risk of cycles of self-blame and guilt that we can fall into when we make mistakes or when we don't spend enough time with our children. An awareness of our mistakes or the need to spend more quality time with our children can be constructive, as it can lead us to want to change things. But if we become so stressed by our guilt that it affects our mood and our interaction with our children, it can become detrimental to our relationship with them.

Many of these reactions are brought on by parents attempting to measure up to an idealised notion of what 'the perfect parent' is, and then feeling that they have failed.

A good way to avoid these parenting traps is to learn how to recognise them when they arise, being a little more forgiving (of yourself, your partner and your children) and then focusing on taking good care of yourself.

It could be anything from giving yourself time, whether alone or with friends, remembering to pursue what matters to you, whether it means going back to work, organising trips, gallery visits or a walk in the park. And, of course, taking good care of ourselves includes acknowledging the times when we feel so overwhelmed that we need to ask for help.

Why this works?

When we take good care of ourselves, we also feel better about the world because taking time to look after our own needs makes us feel regenerated, relaxed and better able to look after others. The added bonus of such a restoration of energy and sense of self is that the rest of the family will also benefit from it. For when we thrive, so do the rest of the family, our 'happier' and revitalised state enthusing and inspiring both our partner and our children. And when we take care of ourselves they learn to do the same for themselves - a win-win situation!

How to take good care of yourself:

- Give yourself some 'me' time. Sometimes we are so consumed in our role as parents that we drive ourselves into the ground, or just forget to attend to our own needs. There's no use in martyring yourself, as not only will you be a poor role model, but you will also miss out on the most pleasurable aspects of parenting.
- Identify what is important to you and what activities are likely to relax you and help you recharge your batteries (e.g. sports, museums, nights out, etc.) and make sure that you try to schedule this 'me' time every week. And if you really can't schedule time off, then try to encourage your kids to get involved in some of your daytime hobbies too; you may be pleasantly surprised by how positively children can respond to art, gardening, walking etc.
- Don't be hard on yourself and try not to fall into common parenting traps such as wanting to be the 'perfect' parent, or blaming yourself or your children for things that have gone wrong. It is okay to cut the odd corner or to take some time out and appreciate what you've got.

- When you feel you are getting wound up, take a step back, take a deep breath and continue breathing deeply while noticing your emotions. This should significantly reduce any negative emotions, including frustration and help you to decide upon a more effective response (see tool **Taking a Step Back**).
- Use the 'Mindful Breathing' technique described in tool **Taking a Step Back** regularly.
- Always remember that **you have the choice** to react in an effective and positive way, whatever the circumstance - and even when your buttons are pushed.
- Use the **'I feel' Messages** and **Energy Drain** tools from our Toolbox to make sure children understand your limits.
- When you do 'lose it', don't get caught up in self-recrimination, remember that you always have **Rewind and Replay** and **Repairing** at hand.
- Make sure that you find some regular time for laughter with and without the kids.
- Pause and try to have a more 'objective' view of a situation; a bit of humour and self-deprecation can help!).
- Find a parenting pal. It's amazing how often parents feel 'alone' with a problem only to find that other parents are struggling with exactly the same thing.

The voice of the Strict parent:

I believe that while children are one of the most important things in my life, our life as a couple shouldn't entirely revolve around them. And this means being able to take some time out for myself and for my partner without feeling guilty. I therefore used to get very frustrated and angry if my partner cancelled something we had agreed to, just because our kids were getting upset about our going out. However, this reaction used to upset my children even more, so we'd end up going out quite conflicted by these situations and it certainly didn't help our 'dates'. I realised that it was much better to explain to the children the importance of taking time for ourselves, before a tantrum/protest had time to develop (see **Planning Ahead**). Once I felt that they understood why Mummy and Daddy needed 'me-time' too, I was then able to give them lots of empathy over their sadness at our leaving. Of course, our children still sometimes have the occasional emotional outburst when they see us leave, but they now calm down as soon as we walk out of the door because we have helped them reduce their anxiety.

The voice of the All-heart parent:

I used to think that I should sacrifice myself for my kids. So I would often cancel my own plans in order to stay at home with them whenever they became unhappy about my leaving them with someone else. But when I did some research on the matter, I learned that children learn more from what we do than from what we say because they just want to be like us. So I realised that when I did cancel my plans, I was sending the wrong message to them, which is that I was not taking good care of myself. In other words, I was not **Modelling** (see corresponding tool) the kind of behaviour or attitude that I'd have liked them to adopt for themselves. I now focus on showing them, through my own actions, that it is really important to find the right balance between one's own needs and everybody else's. I no longer feel selfish when I take time to do something for myself.

Tool No 17: Being Consistent

> **Use for:** *Setting clear expectations for your child, increasing the likelihood of children respecting the limits that you set, preventing conflicts with your partner, teaching by example.*

The key to success in applying any tool in this toolbox is to be consistent in its application. Indeed, as explained previously, children do what works for them. So, if they find that 'misbehaving' works (for example whining or arguing gets them something that they want because you give in), they will surely repeat this behaviour to try to get something else in the future. The key to breaking this 'cycle' is to be consistent by not giving in and by repeating an 'empathetic statement' (see tool **Diffusing Whining and Arguing**). This will make it clear for your child that you mean what you say.

If we make too many exceptions to the rules that we set and we do not 'enforce' the consequences that we have issued, our child will think that they can get away with it and they will continue displaying the very behaviour that we'd like to change.

We should ideally stick to adhering to a balanced parenting style, as 'oscillating' between being strict and then being lenient a few moments later can unsettle our children and blur the boundaries.

Disclaimer: We are human, which means that we are bound to be inconsistent at times and this makes this one of the hardest tools to implement. However, being conscious of the importance of being consistent and not making too many 'exceptions' can make a significant difference.

Why this works?

Consistency is what allows children to feel more secure and have clear expectations, knowing what is acceptable and unacceptable at all times. Children are bound to test the limits (as it is part of their development), and if they feel that these limits are inconsistent, they will push further to check if parents mean what they are saying, and they will not know when to stop. Being consistent will also ensure that your children trust your word.

How to be consistent:

- Be consistent in your parenting style and try your utmost not to oscillate between being strict and then much more lenient, depending on the time of day and your stress level.
- Respond to whining, nagging and arguing (or any other forms of 'manipulation' tactics) with an empathetic statement and do not give in, as this will otherwise reinforce your children's 'mis'behaviour.
- The idea is not to be totally rigid, but if you decide to make an exception and give in to a demand that you had initially rejected, tell your child that it's an exception so that you are not reinforcing their unacceptable behaviour.
- Give **Limited Choices** as often as possible (and be consistent about it!) as it keeps you on top of the situation, limits conflict and makes everyone feel more respected.
- When you set a rule (see tool **Setting Rules**) and your child breaks this rule, make sure that you follow with a related, reasonable and respectful consequence (see tool **Logical Consequences**). This is particularly important when you start implementing a new tool, as it will ensure that your child understands that you are serious about the (new) rules that you have set.
- When you set a delayed consequence (see tool **Delayed Consequences**), make sure that you apply a consequence at a later time or date (as above, at least the first times that you apply this tool).
- Do not issue empty threats as this undermines your authority. Try instead to focus on what you can control (see tool **'I' Statements**).
- If your child commits to doing something, for e.g. in a problem solving session (see tool **Problem Solving**), and you have agreed to remind them in a certain way of their agreement, make sure that you remind them as this will help them get used to the fact that they need to be responsible for implementing their own decisions.

- Use sticky notes or reminders on your phone to remember all the things that you need to remind your child about, or the delayed consequence that you should not forget to apply.
- And last but certainly not least, be consistent in giving unconditional love to your child.

The voice of the Strict parent:

My partner's lack of consistency is one of my biggest frustrations in my relationship with her. I always try to be as consistent as I can, as I think that it's really important to 'set the tone' and make sure that my kids know that when I say something, I mean it. It therefore really frustrates me that I cannot predict how my partner is going to react to a situation, and that she might 'give in' or let the children get away with something unacceptable.

However, I realised that no one can always be consistent, so I learnt to be more flexible with my wife, my children and even with my myself and to allow for exceptions - but not too often! Now, my 'rigidity' isn't getting in the way of my connection with my children and my spouse.

The voice of the All-heart parent:

This is arguably the most difficult tool for me to follow. Indeed, I like to follow my instincts and I don't like too much rigidity in my relationship with my children. I use to feel that it wasn't worth putting up a fight with my children in order to enforce something that I didn't think would have dire consequences if not done. I have since come to realise that by not being consistent enough, I was not giving my children very clear rules and expectations. I was also feeding my children the idea that if they act in 'unreasonable' ways, they may get what they want. I am still not consistent 100% of the time, but I am doing much better and when I make exceptions - much more rarely than I use to, I now make sure that my kids know that it's an exception so that it doesn't reinforce their 'mis'behaviour.

Summary of 'How to be a good role model to your children'

- It is crucial to realise the impact that your reactions have on your children as you can prevent a lot of issues by reacting differently.
- Remember that you cannot expect your children to control their emotions all the time, as it's often just as difficult for us as adults.
- Children absorb everything around them, especially what we don't want them to hear or see.
- It is natural for children to want to imitate their parent's behaviour and adopt their beliefs (particularly before the age of 12), which is why **Modelling** is such an important tool.
- If you 'model' good manners and the values that you hold most dear, your children are very likely to replicate these qualities themselves.
- Taking good care of yourself not only reduces the stress of parenthood, but also models for your children the importance of a healthy approach to one's own needs and identity.
- Show your children that achieving a good balance in family life means that your needs have to be addressed as well as theirs.
- Don't give in to whining, nagging and arguing (or any other forms of 'manipulation' tactics) - to do so will only reinforce your children's 'mis'behaviour.
- Be as consistent as you can when dealing with your children so that they respect your word.

Your notes:

Coming up in

Chapter 4:

- What a child may be thinking
- Tool No 18: Empathy and Validation
- Tool No 19: Active Listening
- Summary of 'How to listen so children will *want* to talk'

Chapter 4: How to listen so children will *want* to talk

Children need to feel able to talk to their parents about upsetting, embarrassing or scary issues. The ones who don't feel listened to can end up turning inwards and bottling up their worries or fears, or looking for consolation elsewhere as they grow older. They might therefore look for solace in other people, such as their peers - and some may have a negative influence on them.

Knowing how to listen to our children in a way that makes them want to share issues with us can be quite a difficult skill to master, particularly as the kids grow older and become more self-conscious.

A child's willingness to share depends on many things. Some of the key factors involved include:

- Their developing character – are they naturally inclined to be chatty or are they more reserved?

- Their age - children tend to go through 'phases' where they want to share more.

- Whether they feel that we know how to listen to them – as confiding in a parent has to be an enjoyable experience.

We cannot control whether or not our children want to talk to us, but we should always do our best to make them feel that we are here for them, and that we can listen to whatever issue they bring to us without judgement.

As we will see in this chapter, there are a number of key ways to encourage our children to 'open up to us'.

What a child may be thinking

I feel really hurt when my Mum and Dad tell me that I need to stop crying about something that hurts me or makes me sad because they say that "it isn't that serious". I mean how do they know if my knee is really hurting me or not?

I only want to let someone know that I feel upset about something when I know that they care, and are going to listen to what I have to say. Otherwise there's no point in telling them, especially if they are going to make me feel worse. What really annoys me when I tell my parents about something that's bothering me is that they try to take over and fix it their way. So often I don't tell them what's wrong.

Tool No 18: Empathy and Validation

> **Use for:** *Helping your child understand and process emotions, building a connection with your child, reducing power struggles and whining, dealing with tantrums, supporting an upset child, diverting negative emotions.*

We often discount our children's feelings without even realising we are doing it. For example, if our six-year old forgets her ballet bag and is distraught about it, we might say, "Come on, you don't need to worry about a ballet bag, we'll get it tomorrow", failing to realise that what she might hear us say is that her feelings aren't important and have been discounted. It is much more effective to focus on 'connecting' with our distressed child by using empathy to acknowledge their feelings, rather than feel we have to fix things.

Expressing empathy for the emotion they are experiencing (for e.g. "You seem sad to have forgotten your ballet bag"), allows them to know that we are 'tuned in' to them. By 'meeting them where they are' (instead of where we'd like them to be), we allow them to move on from their upset much faster, and it allows us to then offer help in 'redirecting' their emotion. And when we validate our children's feelings, it also allows them to be able to learn how to deal with those emotions, as well as trust themselves and their reactions.

This empathy can be demonstrated both verbally and non-verbally to your child, through such actions as sitting next to your son or daughter and giving them undivided attention, or by just hugging them - which often works wonders.

At times, it may be hard to express empathy, especially when we 'know' that our children are making more of a scene than the situation deserves. We need to realise that this is our judgement of the situation, and even if it doesn't seem important to us, it is to them. The more they feel heard, the more we can assist them to recover from their emotion and the less likely our children will feel the need to overreact in the future.

We may also think that giving them empathy in these circumstances may reinforce their behaviour. Yet children need to have their feelings accepted and respected for them to be able to self-regulate their emotions[27] (see tool **Emotional Resilience**).

We also need to be aware that any judgement we make of a child's perception is our own, and may not correspond to the way he or she thinks or feels at all. It is really important that we give our children enough 'space' to contradict us and tell us what they're really feeling (see tool **Active Listening**).

Why it works:

When we give empathy to our children and validate their feelings, they feel listened to and understood. When they come to us expressing sadness or other feelings, it is usually because they crave connection with us, and the best way we can meet their need is by showing them empathy rather than discounting their feelings. This sense of being heard teaches them in turn how to show empathy towards others, and how to show it towards themselves - a gift for life! When children hear their feelings being validated they are better able to deal with them and are able to 'come out' of difficult states of emotion far quicker, rather than be 'stuck' inside them. When a child is able to understand the difference between their (temporary) emotions and their underlying (permanent) self, they are given the tools to process, rather than be dominated by, an emotion or feeling.

How to give Empathy and Validation:

1. **Don't deny your child his or her feelings or try to save them from it**: don't tell your child: "It's going to be ok" or "Come on, it's not that bad!" or "Calm down".
2. **Do not immediately ask your child "Why are you crying?"**, even if you have no idea why they are in such emotional distress. Much of the time children find it hard to answer this question, and asking it of them doesn't help them process their

emotion. If you really need to because your child is not sharing the reason, you can ask this after following the steps below.

3.   **Meet them 'where they are' by acknowledging your child's feelings and help name their feelings:** Your child may not be able to understand, acknowledge or explain the emotion they are experiencing, therefore you can help them by reading the signs of an emotional state in their behaviour and body language (just as one might look for the tell-tale signs of tiredness). This includes 'negative' emotions such as anger or sadness. Helping them put a name on their emotions enables them to 'own' this feeling, and therefore control it. Words are not only empowering, but they also 'normalise' situations, turning them from an unknown, amorphous mass into something knowable and manageable[28]. For example:

  a. When your child is upset and throwing a tantrum: "You seem really frustrated and angry," or "You seem to have a lot of trouble coping with what I just told you?"

  b. When your child has hurt themselves: "Oh, this must hurt!" or "You seem in a lot of pain, the fall must have been harder than it looked?"

  c. When your child is getting very angry with their sibling: "I can see that this situation is upsetting you".

  d. When your child is confiding in you: encourage them with **Active Listening**.

  e. When your child is misbehaving: always start by giving them empathy and then apply consequences. See tools **Logical Consequences** and **Uh-oh and Time-Away.**

4.   **Help your child redirect their emotions (only once you have done the above).** When your children are younger, a good way to do this is to put them in 'thinking mode':

  a. When your child is upset and throwing a tantrum, you can give them a choice. For example: "Would you like to come with me to your room and play a game or stay here on the floor?"

b. When your child has hurt themselves: "Do you need help getting up or can you do it by yourself?" or "Does this hurt a lot, average or just a bit?" or "Would a hug make you feel better?"

c. When your child is upset with their sibling: "Fighting won't solve the situation, if I were you, I would try using words instead."

d. In most other situations, you can ask your child: "Is there something that I can do to help?"

e. **Give them a hug:** keep in mind that giving our children hugs is an essential way to redirect their emotions and to demonstrate our love to them - some psychologists go as far as saying that we need to give a minimum of 12 hugs a day to our children for them to thrive.

NB: The more you practice the above, the faster your child will be able to deal with their emotions. It is therefore really worth taking the extra time to help children process their emotions from the earliest age, as you will both reap the benefits later.

Also worth noting is that as your child grows older (we would say from the age of seven), they are in a better position to understand their feelings and it can be better not to make an assumption about what they're feeling. Instead, you can start making more general statements rather than try to name their feelings, such as "Seems like you are having strong emotions, do you want to talk about it?"

The voice of the Strict parent:

I grew up believing that when a child is behaving badly, the worst thing you can do is to show them empathy because it will only reinforce their 'naughty' or emotional behaviour. This is why I fell in to the trap of trying to toughen up my children by saying things like: "Come on, it's not that bad". Now I realise that such tactics, rather than being helpful, were actually discounting my children's feelings, which didn't help them either to trust their feelings or to be able to recover from them.

The voice of the All-heart parent:

As I don't like to see my children suffer or experience emotional distress of any kind, my reflex reaction was to give them lots of love, but at the same time offer constant reassurance, thinking it would reduce their pain. What I hadn't accounted for was that by telling them it was 'going to be ok', or 'it wasn't so bad' my children would feel 'robbed' of their right to feel distressed or hurt. This did not make them feel understood and it taught them little about how to manage their own emotions.

Real Life Example:

What not to do:

While preparing for swimming lessons we heard a mother repeatedly telling her son to stop crying. After the twelfth time of hearing his mother shout "Stop crying!", the boy's tears ended. However, the moment his mother left the side of the pool the tears returned. Clearly his mother's admonishments, rather than addressing the cause of his tears, had merely discounted his feelings to such an extent that he felt unable to express them until she was out of sight. It struck us as a sad example of a child having his feelings ignored and undermined, only for them to resurface again later on.

What to do:

Our middle child Yasmine, aged three, used to dissolve into tears and become inconsolable quite frequently when things did not go her way. At a loss as to how to stem her tears we alternated between trying to toughen her up and reassure her, yet on she'd cry. Once we read about the importance of showing our children empathy when troubled, we decided to show empathy towards Yasmine when she fell and was crying. Then once we'd expressed this empathy, in a statement such as 'That fall must have really hurt", we'd offer her our support e.g. "Do you need help in getting up?", to which she often answered (to our surprise) even if she had bloody knees: "No it's ok, I can get up by myself".

And provided she hadn't been badly hurt, her tears soon dried up and she'd bounce back to cheerfulness. Thanks to our use of Empathy and

Validation, Yasmine was able to change her behaviour - and most probably also her inner beliefs - to such a degree that her uncontrolled weeping and wailing became a thing of the past.

Tool No 19: Active Listening

> *Use for:* *Understanding your child, allowing your child to share important things, building a connection with your child, supporting an upset child, diverting negative emotions.*

When our children share a problem with us (for e.g. "I have no friends at school"), it is a very natural reaction for us to try to give them a solution to this problem or offer reassurances that it's not really that bad. What we don't realise is that this 'natural' reaction tends to have the effect of dismissing, discounting or negating our child's feelings. It also takes away the opportunity for our child to 'own' their problem and try to solve it themselves.

We often underestimate how many problems can be resolved by just allowing our children to be 'heard', rather than rushing to fix it ourselves by offering them solutions and advice. Therefore, instead of jumping into providing solutions or 'taking the problem away' with reassurances, we should first take the time to simply validate and reflect back what we are hearing. It is sometimes quite hard to supress one's 'I will sort this out for you' reflex, but it is a tool well worth practicing because of the short-term and long-term benefits it brings.

Why this works:

Listening is the basis of empathy, and any child (and adult) feels more understood when they feel listened to without judgment, or without having to listen to advice. In other words, they know that the listener hasn't got an agenda beyond giving their undivided attention. This type of dedicated attention is a marvellous way to increase the connection, communication and overall bond between child and parent.

How to do Active Listening

1. When you feel that your child has something important to share, listen quietly and attentively – try sitting side-by-side, shoulder-to-shoulder (eye-to-eye contact can make it more difficult for children to feel comfortable enough to share).

If you feel that they are going through a rough patch and you'd like to talk to them about it, name what you think they may be feeling, and ask them if they would like to talk about it. For example: "You seem to be a bit sad today, do you want to talk about it?"

2. While they are sharing, refrain from:
    a) Judging, giving advice and solutions.
    b) Discounting your child's feelings by reassuring them that "It's not that bad."

3. Show your child that you are listening:
    a) Repeat what your child is saying or rephrase it (as your children grow older you will increasingly need to rephrase what they have said because a direct repetition might be misinterpreted as sarcasm; or
    b) Validate their feelings with EMPATHY by describing how you think your child might be feeling: e.g. "That sounds painful...", or "Sounds like you are feeling upset..."
    c) Do not 'exaggerate' their feelings (i.e. try and use the same tone as they are using and do not use superlatives) as this could make them doubt your sincerity.

4. Don't try to 'fix' the problem, and remember that the way we say things and use our body language matters more than the words we use.

5. The techniques described above will help our child to process their emotions, and will often be enough for them to get rid of their negative feelings. However, in some cases they may be coming to you with an issue that they would like you to offer direct support on. In these cases, once you have really heard everything that they have to say, you can use the tool **Generating Solutions**, to coach them into finding their own solutions to their challenges.

    NB: If you have a child who doesn't naturally share things with you, you will need to give them a 'nudge'. We recommend steering away from open questions such as "What is happening to you?" or "How was school today?" (unless you just want to hear "Good" or "Ok").

Also, avoid putting pressure on your children by using statements such as "I can see that something is bothering you, you need to tell me about it so that I can help you."

Instead, try and ask more specific questions or to simply name what you are seeing. For example:

- "You seem to be bothered by something, do you want to talk about it?" - (if they say that they don't want to talk about it, don't insist, just let them know that you are here for them any time that they *would* like to have a chat).

- When your child comes back from school, ask specific questions like "What was your best (or worse) moment at school today?" or "What is the one thing that you learnt today at school that you really liked/were interested in?", etc.

The voice of the Strict parent:

I wasn't very good at taking time to sit down and 'listen' to my kids (particularly when they were younger than six), preferring to spend our time together on activities. But once I discovered the importance of listening in an active and reflective way, I spent a lot of time using this tool with my kids because amazing things come out of these sessions.

The voice of the All-heart parent:

I like to give my kids attention, so it comes naturally to me to listen to them and ask a lot of questions. However, I realised that my questions were often too 'cerebral' for them to be able to answer (for e.g. "Why do you think your friend reacted like this?"). And I was too quick to reassure, or help find solutions, which often took away the space for them to talk about how they felt and made them feel undermined or frustrated.

Real Life Example:

What not to do:

Sonia's daughter Lara comes back from school today looking sad.

"Oh Mum, during break time some of the girls are being mean to me."

Only half listening to what her daughter is saying to her and how she is saying it, Sonia answers:

"Never mind darling, they are probably only playing and being silly, I wouldn't worry about it."

"But they are really bothering me, Mum!" Lara insists.

"Well I'd just tell them to be nice to you from now on, they will soon stop."

During the following weeks, Lara started to wake up at night asking for comfort food when she wouldn't eat properly during meals, and started to become more difficult with completing homework. Failing to make a connection between Lara's behaviour and her earlier complaint, Sonia gets frustrated with her daughter's increasing unmanageability and repeatedly tells her off.

It isn't until Sonia is approached by Sophie's mother, a friend of Lara's, that Sonia begins to realise her error.

"Sophie is so upset by the cruel way those girls are ganging up on Lara that she is having nightmares about the whole thing!" the other mother says.

"What do you mean cruel games?" asks Sonia, alarmed, "What's been happening?"

"You mean Lara didn't tell you about the "Let's kill Lara" game that's been going on during break times?"

With horror, Sophie realises that yes, Lara had tried to confide in her mother about the horrible time she was having at school, but rather than really listening to her daughter's distress, Sonia had tried to 'help' her by minimising and telling her it was not that bad.

Summary of 'How to listen so children will *want* to talk'

- Listen to your children and 'tune in' to their emotions, as this will make them far more willing to share their feelings with you (particularly during difficult moments).
- Empathy is probably the single most important thing that you can give your children.
- Giving your children empathy whatever the circumstance - and yes this can sometimes feel very difficult - allows you to connect with your children and demonstrate your unconditional love for them.
- Giving your children empathy helps them trust their feelings and be able to process their emotional distress faster.
- When your children cry or show other signs of emotional distress, try not to immediately save them from their distress by telling them that everything is ok. And telling them that there is no reason to cry minimises their feelings and makes them feel discounted.
- 'Actively' listen to your children (as often as possible).
- Active and reflective listening requires you to just repeat or to summarise what your children are saying to you, without any comments and without immediately giving them solutions to the issues that they are sharing with you.

You notes

Your notes

Coming up in

Chapter 5:

- What a child may be thinking
- Tool No 20: Effective Communication
- Tool No 21: Acknowledgement and Encouragement
- Tool No 22: 'I feel' Messages
- Summary of 'How to talk so children will *want* to listen'

Chapter 5: How to talk so children will *want* to listen

It has to be the most common complaint heard by parents: "Why won't my children do what I say the first time I ask them? Why do my words seem to fall on deaf ears?". The need to get our children to listen to us, and act on what we say, is so fundamental to our sense of parenting success that the search for a solution represents something of a hunt for the Holy Grail.

Fortunately, you need look no further than the following chapters (5, 6 and 7) for easy-to-use solutions to get your child to listen to you, and become more willing to comply with your requests.

🎈 What a child may be thinking

All I hear from Mum and Dad is "Do this, do that", or "You mustn't!" … "You can't!"… "Why didn't you…?" My father usually tells me what to do by shouting it, and my Mum usually nags me and begs me to do things. They don't seem to feel that I'm important enough to have a choice in what I'm allowed to do. They nag me so much that I just want to show them that I can have my say by saying "No" or by ignoring them.

If I go on for long enough about something and don't do it or insist on getting something, my Mum will usually give in, so this works for me. When I try to do this with my father, he gets really cross, but at least he pays attention to me and I love being able to control his tone of voice!

Tool No 20: Effective Communication

> **Use for:** *Replacing yelling, nagging and reminding, increasing the chances of being listened to by your child, building a connection with your child, correcting misbehaviours, reducing power struggles and whining, diverting negative emotions, building self-esteem, encouraging responsibility and social skills.*

Sometimes children just won't listen to us, regardless of how nicely we ask them, which can make us feel that the only way to 'get through' to them is by raising our voices. Unfortunately, as soon as children are yelled at, they go into 'fight or flight' mode and the part of their brain that is able to reason - the 'pre-frontal cortex' - shuts down, which makes them even less likely to listen to us. Of course, they may end up doing what we shouted at them to do, but only out of fear and not out of understanding or conviction. And that is why parents who do yell to get themselves heard will find that they need to do it regularly, because children are not 'learning' the lesson or the reason why it should be done.

It's normal for us to become impatient with our children, especially when they 'push our buttons'. Typically, in the rough and tumble of everyday life, we are so 'up against it' that we forget to treat our kids in the way we would wish to be treated ourselves. We cannot expect our children to learn to control their emotions if we don't show them that we're capable of controlling ours. It is thus really important to try to keep our communication with them as respectful and composed as possible. Thankfully, there are many tips for how to communicate with them in a respectful and effective way and still get their attention.

We should ideally coach our children from an early age to use respectful communication through modelling this behaviour to them at all times (see tool **Modelling**). Indeed, when a child, or for that matter an adult, is screamed at, they are likely to learn that it is ok for them to scream at others. Since these habits become ingrained over time, it becomes more difficult for children to give up 'rude' forms of communication because they have seen them 'modelled'.

So, when attempting to change this pattern of behaviour (and all others) by steering our children in a new direction, it is important to do so with empathy and not be too harsh. This is done by gradually coaching our children (as well as ourselves) in the art of being more mindful and considerate of the way we speak to each other, accentuating the positive and reducing the negative. Fortunately, once the whole family are committed to change, it doesn't take too long for the 'Do as you would be done by message' to start working in practice.

Why it works:

Human beings would rather be treated respectfully, and are more likely to do things if they are asked in a respectful way. This guiding principle obviously applies to children as well as adults, yet it is still so easy to forget this consideration when children start being uncooperative in the middle of a busy day.

How to use Effective Communication:

- **Respect breeds respect:** be as polite to your children as you can possibly be and avoid shouting whenever possible.
- **Speak to them when you're close to them:** Try not to call out from a distance, unless in an emergency (if you have to shout out an instruction make sure it is done so in a friendly voice and without anger). Instead, come close to your child, get down to their level, try to make eye contact with them (but be aware that they may not be ready for this so don't force it), and speak to them softly. Or even better **whisper**, as whispering usually has very positive effects on children.
- **Allow some time** for them to do what you ask: Try as much as possible to leave a bit of time for your children to finish what they are doing or just to carry out your requests. A good tactic is to ask them whether they want to do what you have asked now or in five minutes (See tool **<u>Limited Choices</u>**).

- **Try not to use many reminders and nagging**. When you are talking to your child ask yourself: "Is this new information that I am giving?" If it isn't (and it is often the case!), then you should use the tool **Asking Questions**.
- **Try not to do too much 'explaining'**, particularly when there is tension in the air. The more words we use, the less effective we become.
- **Do not 'box' them or 'label' them:** Labelling your children 'naughty', 'bad boy/girl', 'the challenging one', 'over-sensitive', 'cry baby', etc. can backfire as it can encourage them to take on this identity. You need to allow children to develop their own identity, rather than 'boxing' them into one, particularly in the early years. Even using more positive labels such as 'good' or 'smart' is a judgement and can be detrimental in the long term as children can become afraid of 'losing' this label (See tool **Acknowledgement and Encouragement**).
- **Do not compare them**: Try and never compare them to their siblings (even if it's tempting to take the example of the one who is doing just what you've asked, while the other one is being more challenging), or to other friends.

  NB: If your children aren't listening to you, and this has become a regular issue, look in the trouble-shooting section to the solution to 'Ignoring me' and read the tool **Problem Solving** and the example at the end of it.

The voice of the Strict parent:

When I read the research revealing that yelling was not only ineffectual, but was actually detrimental, I found it hard to believe because it seemed counterintuitive. For me, shouting at my children seemed the most effective and direct way of getting them to listen to me, particularly when they seemed unwilling to cooperate. And then one day, my eldest daughter started shouting orders back at me. I was really shocked that she'd been so rude, and my gut reaction was to respond very harshly to make sure I nipped this behaviour in the bud. However, once I calmed down, it dawned on me that she had simply spoken to me in the way I often spoke to her. In other words, she had learned through my behaviour that shouting at someone was an acceptable form of communication. Now I use the Effective Communication tool, and others in this toolbox, to make sure that I don't need to raise my voice to make myself heard.

The voice of the All-heart parent:

Although I wanted very much to communicate respectfully with my kids, I realised that my inherited methods left much to be desired since I was often repeating myself. This was clearly not an effective strategy, particularly since my children were getting used to the idea that I would be reminding them about something several times before I actually did anything about it. I've learnt to engage their thinking and enlist their desire to have some control over their lives with the tools that we have found. I can see that it works, and my daughters also use these forms of communication amongst themselves to get themselves heard or get what they want.

⊗ Tool No 21: Acknowledgement and Encouragement

> **Use for:** *Replacing 'evaluative praise' and 'constructive criticism', building self-esteem and self-evaluation, offering feedback, encouraging your child to try new things, developing empathy.*

Raising our children's self-esteem is one of our key goals as parents. One of the most effective methods of encouraging our children to develop a sense of self-esteem is by 'modelling' positive interaction with them (see tool **Modelling**). Self-esteem is also about embracing 'self-responsibility' - the knowledge and confidence our children gain by knowing that they can overcome challenges without relying on another's intervention or praise.

Research shows that 80% of parents' interaction with their children is based around negative comments and criticism, observations that are often made unconsciously. Since children naturally crave our acceptance and appreciation, they are likely to internalise our negative remarks as feelings of not being 'good enough' or as having failed in some way. The best way that we can guard against our children losing their self-esteem, is for us to make a conscious effort to convert our negative comments into more positive and encouraging remarks.

In order to do this, it is crucial to manage our expectations of what our children are able to achieve at different ages. Indeed, over-expectation can easily lead children to feel that whatever they do is never 'good enough'. Children can easily develop this form of low self-esteem when criticised, even if the criticism appears to be 'constructive', including showing how something could have been done better.

That said, it is also important not to 'over-praise' our children with general statements such as "This is great!" or "You're so clever!" Because as they soon spot that we are so hopelessly biased that we will admire just about everything they do, or that we are just insincere in our appreciation, our praise becomes meaningless.

Also, extensive research has proven that praising our children with 'evaluative' words such as 'good' or 'clever" can actually make them become afraid of failure[29], although this may sound counterintuitive. Indeed, children become afraid of not living up to the expectations set by our words of praise, and therefore become more risk-averse as they want to make sure that they won't disappoint us. So, instead of praising our children with general/evaluative words, it is more effective to acknowledge their effort, behaviour or even their attitude. Praising specific aspects of their achievement in this way will help them learn to self-evaluate their abilities in the future. So, for example, telling your child "You've done really well, you must have put a lot of effort in this", is much more valuable than another "You've done well, you're really smart".

Often just describing something that your child has achieved, or expressing interest in the achievement by asking a question about how they did it, is the best way to praise a child. So for example saying, "I really like the way you mixed the colours in your picture", is better than, "That's a lovely picture". When we show our children that their work is interesting, it enables them to 'self-evaluate' in future rather than become dependent on our opinion or judgement.

Finally, 'staged' eavesdropping - for example praising our child to a partner or another adult within their hearing but not deliberately in front of them - can also be a great way to acknowledge a child.

Why it works:

Children naturally crave our acceptance and appreciation, which means that the way we comment on their actions and achievements will influence their self-esteem. If we make too many negative comments, it will most likely affect their self-esteem negatively. Conversely, if we 'over-praise' our children, they will become 'praise or approval junkies', people who are unable to value their own work unless someone else is on hand to give their seal of approval. Our role as parents is to encourage our children with 'descriptive praise' rather than evaluative praise, and to help them learn to self-evaluate their abilities.

How to use Acknowledgement and Encouragement.

- **Praise the effort:** For e.g. "I can see by your playing how much you have practiced." When we focus on our children's effort, rather than their achievement, we encourage them to learn the art of motivation and self-evaluation: "Yes, I worked really hard to get to this result so it's worth making the effort in the future".

- **Praise descriptively rather than using 'evaluative' praise:** Instead of saying "Wow, this is so beautiful!" ask your child a question e.g. "How did you do this part?", or describe what you see, e.g. "Wow the chicken in your drawing looks so lifelike!" Your child will appreciate that you have taken an interest in his or her work, and how it was executed, and is more likely to realise his or her achievements and want to talk about it.

- **Praise specific actions rather than their overall behaviour:** This allows your child to realise that their behaviour is something that they *choose* rather than something they *are*. For e.g. instead of saying "You behaved really well when Granny was here", you can say, "I really appreciated that you helped Granny get in and out of her chair during her visit."

- **Make it about them:** What we ultimately want is for our children to develop their own power of self-evaluation, rather than become 'praise junkies', dependent on us to tell them if they are doing well. Instead of "I'm so proud of you", you can help them realise their own achievements by asking them instead "You have worked hard and did well on this test, are you proud of yourself?", or "Are you happy with the result?", and once they answer, "Yes I am", you can always add: "I am proud of you too!"

- **Be selective in your praise**: Praise everything your child does and he or she will either discount what you are saying or become dependent on praise for self-affirmation. Don't overdo it. However, some people have a tendency to 'under-praise' in fear that this might 'spoil' their child. Be aware that this is not good either, as our children need our encouragements and positive comments to feel good about what they do.

- **Accentuate the positive, reduce the negative:** Make sure that your positives outweigh the negatives so that you fill your child's 'I'm capable account' instead of filling the 'I'm a failure account'. Research shows that children need at least three times more positive comments than negative ones. For example, rather than saying "No, that's not the way to do this", suggest for e.g. "I see that you've done it this way. There's another way of doing it that you might prefer, shall I show it to you?"
- **Try not to criticise:** Even 'constructive criticism' can be interpreted by your child as being negative. You need to always try to identify the good things in something that your child has done and ask the child to explain the reason for their success (usually the effort that they've put into it). This helps fill the 'I'm capable account'. If you feel that there is room for improvement, you can then add: "What could you better next time?"
- **Be honest:** Even young kids can see right through false praise. It is important to remain honest. If you're not impressed by your child's achievement, you don't have to label their action as good or bad and can just mention something like: "I see that you're practicing your violin." This just lets your child know that they have your attention.
- **Let your child eavesdrop:** make sure your child overhears you praising to your partner or friend something that your child did (but don't overdo it as boastful parents are rarely popular and kids can get embarrassed).
- **You don't always need to say something:** Sometimes giving them a smile or a hug can be more powerful than using words.

The voice of the Strict parent:

I used to believe that expressing 'constructive criticism' was a good way of guiding and instructing my children (for e.g. "Yes this is good, but you could've done this bit better"). Yet once I realised that the majority of my comments to them were actually rather negative, I managed to turn things around by finding positive things to say whatever the outcome. I also started encouraging my children to learn the art of 'self-evaluation' by asking questions such as: "Are you feeling proud of what you achieved?" instead of just giving my own evaluation of their achievements.

The voice of the All-heart parent:

Like so many parents, I believed that heaping the praise on to my children was a good way of nurturing them and building their self-confidence. So I was fascinated to discover how 'blanket' praise is of little use to children. I also learned that good self-esteem comes from our children overcoming challenges, and not from hearing parents dish out praise at every opportunity. From then on, I made sure that I concentrated on giving my children helpful, descriptive praise, which focused on their ability to make the right decision. I also made sure that I asked them lots about the 'process', the way they made or created something.

Real Life Example:

Once I (Nadim) realised how important it is to teach a child to be able to evaluate their own efforts and achievements, I started using the phrase "You must be proud of yourself!" on my six-year-old daughter Noor, whenever she'd done something to deserve it. Initially, she didn't seem to recognise the importance of this feeling and brushed it off, often responding "It was easy", making me feel dubious about whether this technique worked. Then six months later she came back from ballet one day and said,

"Oh Dad I was named ballerina of the week today."

To which I replied in my usual way, "Hey you must be proud of yourself!"

To which she responded, "Yes I am proud of myself, I practiced a lot to get this award!"

At that moment, I realised that all those times when I thought she was ignoring my saying "You must be proud of yourself", she'd actually been slowly incorporating my question into her thought processes until she was ready to use it herself. And from then on she always linked the importance of the effort with the achievement, an invaluable lesson for life.

So don't worry if initially your efforts to acknowledge and encourage your child (rather than praise them indiscriminately) don't seem to be getting the response you'd hoped for, your child is likely to be taking your words on board in silence until the time is right.

Tool No 22: 'I feel' Messages

> **Use for:** *Replacing blame and criticism, teaching our children about feelings and about the effect of their actions on others, giving feedback, setting values, teaching our children, building empathy, diverting misbehaviour.*

'I feel' messages allow us to communicate positively with our children, rather than appearing to question our child's character or personality (which can often happen unintentionally when we talk to our children). Through the 'I feel' Message, we can explain to our children how their behaviour is affecting us and what our needs now are. For example, rather than us saying "Stop shouting!", or "How dare you shout at your mother", we can say "When you shout at me the way you just did, I feel sad and hurt".

Why this works

The 'I feel' Message is a tool based on the theory of 'non-violent communication'[30]. It is used to enable people to communicate without blame or shame, the downside of which is that it puts the listener in a 'defensive' mode. It encourages our child to identify with what we are experiencing, a first and very valuable stage in getting a child to modify his or her behaviour.

How to use 'I feel' messages:

Tell your child how his or her unacceptable behaviour makes you feel in four steps:

1. Describe the unacceptable behaviour "When you are shouting at me..."
2. Explain what we feel: "... I feel hurt" (different from 'it upsets me').
3. Explain the tangible and concrete effect that your child's behaviour has on you e.g. "When you shout at me like that, I feel hurt and it means that I cannot give you the most positive attention". Always keep the sentence in the present tense, as we

want our children to feel that we are addressing a specific issue, rather than 'amalgamating' past issues.

4. (Optional): suggest positive alternative modes of behaviour (using limited choices), for e.g. "Instead of shouting, would you like to whisper with me or speak in your normal voice?"

Other Examples:

"When you speak to me like this, I feel disrespected. I need you to speak to me in a different tone of voice."

"When you pull my sleeve, it damages my jumper and this upsets me. If you want me to listen to you while I'm doing something else, you can put your hand over mine to let me know you have something to say."

The voice of the Strict parent:

Men aren't often encouraged to speak about their feelings, and I was no exception. I thought that speaking to my children about my feelings could make me sound weak, which might undermine their confidence in me as their father. I now realise that letting my children know how I feel about a particular situation helps them become more empathetic and self-aware, and gives them an opportunity to modify their behaviour. But I must admit that I have to keep reminding myself to follow the steps to the 'I feel' Messages, as expressing myself in this way still doesn't come naturally!

The voice of the All-heart parent:

Expressing my emotions has never been a problem for me; I just had to learn how to channel my verbalisation in such a way that my children felt supported by my 'admissions' rather than blamed, shamed or frightened by an over-emotional parent. Using an 'I feel' message is a good example of how one can have a more practical, structured and less chaotic route to allowing your children to know what's in your own heart. It's also useful to convey feelings without blame to one's partner...and I do when I remember to.

Summary of 'How to talk so children will *want* to listen'

- Children will often 'tune their parents out' (particularly as they grow older) because they get bored of hearing the same thing over and over again.
- Asking yourself 'Is this new information?' will help you realise if you are repeating yourself.
- Replace reminding and nagging with tools from this Toolbox, such as **Asking Questions**.
- You need to model the kind of communication skills that you would like your children to reproduce.
- Respect breeds respect, and negativity breeds negativity; children will end up imitating whatever you do (including shouting, getting angry and swearing).
- Children's self-esteem is raised when they are able to overcome challenges for themselves.
- Praise your children for their efforts, and use descriptive rather than general or 'evaluative' praise.
- Make your praise about them and their efforts, rather than your own feelings or your evaluation of what they've done.
- When you use **'I Feel' Messages,** you are encouraging your children to appreciate that others have needs too. This lesson in the importance of empathy leads them (more often than not!) to want to please you.

What you should avoid and what you can now choose to do instead:

Avoid:	Replace with:
Raising your voice from other side of room to be heard	Getting down to their level, whispering
Shouting/screaming	Effective Communication, Diffusing Whining and Arguing, Rewind and Replay, Consequences (see next chapter).
Classifying them in a role, labelling them with a particular characteristic e.g. 'lazy' or 'funny' or comparing them to siblings	Eavesdropping, thinking out loud
Lecturing them	Positive statements (in the third person), 'I' Statements

You notes

Your notes

Coming up in

Chapter 6:

- What a child may be thinking
- Tool No 23: Setting Rules
- Tool No 24: Logical consequences
- Tool No 25: Uh-oh and Time-Away
- Tool No 26: Delayed Consequences
- Tool No 27: Energy Drain
- Summary of 'How to effectively deal with 'mis'behaviour'

Chapter 6: How to effectively deal with 'mis'behaviour

In order to get children to do something that we want them to, it is common for parents to resort to pleading, nagging, threatening, or even yelling (especially when we lose patience).

Unfortunately, threats, reminders and particularly anger, tend to have adverse effects on children, including:

- Feeding misbehaviour

- Inhibiting the growth of our children's self-responsibility because they assume that there will always be someone to remind them about the rules and what needs to be done.

- Causing our children to become addicted to warnings rather than thinking for themselves.

The more our children get used to hearing us issue multiple warnings, reminders and/threats before we actually act on them, the less likely our children are to obey or even react to us the first time around - on the assumption that they still have some time before the ultimate threat is issued. In other words, if we make a threat and fail to act on it, it becomes an empty threat.

Children need to learn that in real life, we seldom get several warnings before we face a consequence. For example, do you get three warnings before getting a ticket for speeding?

The tools in this chapter will focus on making sure that your words are not only heard by your children, but also respected (and acted on) the first time round.

This chapter also tries to shed some light on the significant difference between traditional 'punishment' and its negative effect, and the positive power of 'consequences', which encourages children to be accountable for their own actions.

Punishment is an entirely negative experience because it adds an overlay of shame and guilt that will only create resentment and make future behaviour worse. It teaches children to act from fear instead of acting from love. It models using force instead of compassion. It models hurting another instead of managing our own emotions.[31]

As Jane Nelsen from Positive Discipline has summarised so well: **Children don't need to be made to feel worse in order to do better.**[32]

So instead of using suffering/punishment in order to teach a lesson, we need to encourage children to experience the consequence of their behaviour so that they will always be made accountable for their own choices (see following tools for clarification).

What a child may be thinking

There are so many rules in my life, it's really frustrating! Everything seems to have to be done exactly like my parents wants. How can I remember all of what is asked from me?

I sometimes make mistakes and forget how to behave, or just don't care as much as I should. But I feel that it isn't really fair to keep going on at me, or getting mad and punishing me and generally making me feel rubbish.

Sometimes I get so angry that I get in a huge rage and want to hit somebody. The other day, my Dad got so mad at me for hitting my little brother that he smacked me. But that really confused me because if hitting is wrong, why would you want to hit someone for hitting someone else? In fact, being hit and shouted at just made me even more furious, and a bit frightened from then on because I didn't know when I was going to be smacked and shouted at again. I know that when I get really cross it can be really hard for me to calm down. I'd be much happier if my Mum and Dad tried to help me calm down rather than their getting angry and 'shouty' too.

Tool No 23: Setting Rules

> **Use for:** *Replacing threats, establishing boundaries and foundations for family and personal life, clarifying expectations, improving communication, fostering responsibility, preventing misbehaviour, addressing defiance, bedtimes, mealtimes, homework, outings.*

As the latest research in neuroscience shows[33], our children need boundaries (particularly when they are younger). Boundaries are desirable because an awareness of limits brings a feeling of safety, security and certainty. Indeed, limits help our children develop a healthy sense of 'inhibition', a guide to what is and isn't appropriate, as well as a clarification of what we, and often the rest of the world, expect from them (which may be obvious to us but can sometimes be lost in translation!).

The most important thing to remember is that we need to set limits in ways that can create cooperation rather than power struggles. The trick is to set rules in a non-confrontational way, using the third person and trying to keep the statement positive so that it doesn't sound like a threat, for e.g. "Children who want to eat have to remain seated at the table", instead of: "If you don't stay at the table while we're having dinner, dinner is over for you."

Why this works?

Children (and even adults!) need to understand what we expect from them. They learn early on that there are rules at school as well the outside world, but it is also important for them to appreciate that there are home rules that are equally important. Set rules at home in the same kind of way as they would be set outside the house. Children are much more likely to follow rules that are clear, set in a positive and non-confrontational way (instead of being set as a threat) and that, ideally, apply to everyone in the family.

How to set rules:

- Define House Rules (acceptable vs. unacceptable behaviours to be discussed with spouse and/or other family members).
- 'KISS' (Keep It Short and Simple.)
- Express the rule in the third person.
- Do not use disguised threats.
- Try and keep the statement positive.
- If you are setting a rule for the first time, you can use: "The new rule in this house is ..."
- Once you have set a clear rule, it is useful to ask children to repeat it by asking them: "What is the new rule?"
- If your children break the rule, remember that actions speak louder than words (i.e. keep your words to a minimum) and apply a 'logical consequence' (see **Logical Consequences**).

Examples:

- Try "Children who want to eat have to remain seated at the table", instead of: "If you don't stay at the table while we're having dinner, dinner is over for you."
- Try "Chairs are for sitting on", rather than "Stop standing on the chair!"
- Try "In this house, children don't hit", rather than "If you hit your brother one more time, you will regret it". Although "Children don't hit" is a negative statement and therefore doesn't have the 'positive twist' recommended for setting rules, the use of the third person still makes it effective and far better than typical threats.

The voice of the Strict parent:

Rules are rules and are to be respected. But did I ever think about how I set these rules and how that would affect the way my children reacted to them? No I didn't! And I suffered the consequence - the frustration of seeing my strict rules frequently being broken. Thankfully, once I rephrased my rules in a straightforward and more positive fashion, my expectations became much clearer and my children consequently responded to them in a far more positive, and often willing, way.

The voice of the All-heart parent:

It wasn't easy for me to set rules because I associated them with a negative restriction on my children's right to feel free to be themselves. But once I saw that - when properly implemented - rules could be the very boundaries and guide ropes that children naturally look for, I became their biggest fan. It's a godsend to have a tool that can help me implement these rules in a non-threatening way and one that actually teaches my children that house rules, as well as all other kinds, are to be respected.

Tool No 24: Logical consequences

> **Use for:** *Replacing punishment, addressing all forms of misbehaviour, making your child accountable for their actions, developing your child's sense of responsibility and understanding of cause and effect, learning through mistakes.*

Although our children need, and often crave, clear limits as we have explained in **Setting Rules**, they also have a tendency to break the rules, as it is natural for them to 'test the limits'. When this happens, many parents are tempted to resort to punishment in order to change their child's behaviour and to 'teach' them a lesson. Unfortunately, punishing children, particularly our own, is usually counterproductive.

There is a lot of evidence that punishment rarely works as an inducement to behave in a more responsible fashion. Moreover, there are many drawbacks to punitive consequences, especially when the punisher uses physical force or shames their child in order to get the message across. Evidence shows that children who are regularly punished will turn to using lies as a means of avoiding punishment in future – driving their behaviour 'underground', and children who are spanked can become increasingly aggressive themselves[34].

Conventional punishment usually puts the parent in the active role and the child in the passive, which can often make the child see themselves as the victim of something that is being *done* to them by their parent. Consequently, children often feel resentful after being punished as in, "I'm really annoyed with Daddy because he's stopped me from playing with the iPad for a week". Which, while being an understandable reaction, is hardly likely to motivate the child to be 'good'.

As the psychologist and author Laura Markham explains[35]: 'Punishment cheats children out of the help they need to manage their emotions. It adds an overlay of shame and guilt that will only make them act worse. It models acting from fear instead of acting from love. It models using force instead of compassion. It models hurting another instead of managing our own emotions.'

That being said, we believe that it is essential for children to be accountable for their own actions and to experience the consequence of their choices. Which brings us to the question of how to encourage children to be accountable without using punishment?

First we have to bear in mind that when our children 'misbehave', it usually means that rather than being 'naughty' for the sake of it, they are just trying to get our attention (even if it is negative attention), or using it to gain more control over their lives. For a child, gaining both attention and control is a means of increasing their sense of belonging and 'significance' (see Understanding why our children's 'mis'behave in Introduction). So when seeking to address children's 'mis'behaviour, it is really important to first try to connect with them by using empathy (see tool **Empathy and Validation**).

Once we have given them empathy, we can make them experience the 'logical' or 'immediate' consequence of their poor choice of behaviour in order to learn from it (as they would in real life). But the real key to implementing successful 'consequences', and to differentiate them from punishments, is to make sure that our children do not feel shamed by the experience. So, focus on the child's poor choice rather than labelling the child himself or herself as 'bad' or 'naughty'. It is also important to address the present and not the past and to avoid issuing lectures, reminders and guilt trips. Indeed, the idea is to deliver the consequence with as much empathy as possible, minimise the number of words we use and to avoid at all costs; "I told you so", anger or sarcasm. *See real-life example below.*

Why this works:

The evidence shows that when children experience punishment for a misbehaviour, their attention turns away from a desire to be 'good' and towards avoiding experiencing the punishment again in the future. In other words, rather than wanting to becoming more self-disciplined and obedient, they focus on making sure that their misbehaviour is hidden from their parent's view.

Children react much better if our reaction to their poor choice of behaviour begins with an expression of empathy towards their having made this decision. We can then follow this with a 'logical' consequence, one that does not include blame or shame and follows the three R's rule (see Related, Respectful, Reasonable outlined below).

When we show empathy and respect for our children, shifting our focus away from the child and towards the child's choice, they feel much more willing to take responsibility for their future behaviour. So for example, the child will now think "When I decide to break the rules, it makes everyone unhappy, so I'm better off respecting them from now on". Far better for a child to feel empowered into wanting to change, than backed into a corner and ready to lash out again.

How to use Logical Consequences:

1. A clear limit and expectation must be set before delivering a consequence (see tool **Setting Rules**)

2. Give **empathy first** and then deliver the consequence:
   - Example: say "This is sad", and then deliver the consequence. For e.g. instead of "I told you five times to clean your room and you haven't, so I'm not going to take you to the park! ", try "It's really sad, it seems that you're going to have to stay at home to clean your room."
   - The most 'appropriate' consequence for children making a mess or breaking something is to clean it up themselves (we would always advocate children cleaning up their own mess from the age of two) or paying (at least partly) for something that they break (if they receive an allowance).
   - Appropriate consequences are distinct from punishment because they:
     - Follow the three R's rule: they need to be Related (to the 'mistake' the child has made), Respectful and Reasonable.
     - Are delivered with love and without anger.
     - Fit the misbehaviour.

- Focus on the poor choice and not on the 'bad child'.
- Address the present not the past.
- Are not accompanied by lectures, reminders or a 'guilt trip'.
- Teach your child wisdom by allowing their decision to be the 'bad guy'.

3. Refrain from giving lots of explanations - the more justifications you give for making a particular decision, the more opportunities your child has for arguing with them.

4. Once you have delivered the consequence, you need to 'Stick to your guns', unless you realise that your consequence did not follow the three R's. If this is the case, then don't hesitate to explain to your child that you made a mistake in the heat of the moment and will think of a more appropriate consequence.

The voice of the Strict parent:

I inherited from my parents the belief that punishment was the most effective way to teach children a 'lesson' and change their behaviour. But while my strict parenting methods might lead my children to obey me in the short term, they were usually motivated by fear, which was likely to lead to resentment later on. The evidence, I discovered, was clear: punishment (particularly carried out in anger) damages a parent's connection with their child, rather than giving children an incentive to make genuine changes to their behaviour. Whereas teaching a child to understand how poor choices have logical consequences is a far more effective long-term lesson, and is much more likely to teach them self-discipline and self-control.

The voice of the All-heart parent:

The whole idea of punishing my children caused me pain: I couldn't bear to hurt them and I didn't believe that this was the way to change their behaviour for the better. So of course, I hated it when my partner used punitive techniques on our children. In fact, the combination of his punishments, our children's resentment and the distress I then suffered had a very negative effect on the dynamics at home. I realised that I had to learn how to be both kind and firm at the same time, and to explain, with limited words and without blame or shame, when a behaviour is unacceptable. Thankfully, I am now able to use Logical Consequences to show my children the importance of taking responsibility for their behaviour.

Real Life Example:

At the age of four our daughter Noor, kept leaving the meal table before she had finished eating, assuming that she could return to her food whenever she liked. We tried reasoning with her, explaining to her "We'd really like you to stay at the table so that we can all have breakfast/lunch/supper together", threatening her with all sorts of punishments if she didn't stay put. But to no avail, for off she drifted once more. So we decided to try something different by setting a new rule (see tool Setting Rules) and told Noor: "Children who want to eat need to remain seated at the table" so that she could fully understand the terms of the mealtime. The next time she upped and left without permission, we took her plate and placemat away.

On her return she was inconsolable, but instead of giving in and allowing her to resume eating, which would have made the rule null and void, we held our ground, offering her empathy (rather than 'I told you so's') for her distress, but not returning her missing food. Having understood the consequences of breaking a rule, Noor now remains at the table until she has finished the meal and signals that she has finished by removing her plate herself. In the rare cases where she does get up before finishing, we just need to ask her: "Have you finished your meal?" and if she hasn't, she smiles knowingly and sits back down without argument.

Of course it may seem hard, even painful, to stand your ground the first time your child breaks a rule, particularly if they are distressed. But provided that the consequence is logical, as opposed to disproportionate or unrelated to the transgression, and respectfully applied, the short-term pain is soon alleviated by the long-term effectiveness of the learning.

✖ Tool No 25: Uh-oh and Time-Away[36]

> **Use for:** *Dealing with a child breaking a rule, dealing with violence such as hitting and biting, diffusing angry situations, redirecting behaviour, calming down, encouraging self-soothing, developing responsibility.*

'Uh-oh and Time-Away' is a very specific tool designed to teach our children how to 'pause' and then redirect their behaviour. It is designed to be used specifically when our children (and in some instances ourselves!) need to calm down or just chill out before they (or we) can be asked to make a reasonable decision. It is not a tool for children who are having a tantrum (see the solutions to this challenge in our trouble-shooting section), nor is it a tool for dealing with typical daily power struggles.

A recent and damaging parenting trend has been the recommendation that parents use the 'naughty step' or 'naughty corner' as a way of teaching a child a lesson. Labelling a child naughty is never constructive as it can be 'self-reinforcing', leading the child to identify itself as naughty. Also, shaming a child in this way by excluding them in a punitive fashion is hurtful and can breed resentment. It is therefore crucial, that any parent who wishes to use 'Uh-oh and Time-Away' understands that these tools are neither to be used 'punitively', nor are they 'routine' solutions for correcting everyday behaviour. You will have hopefully read several other alternative tools within our Toolbox for addressing these more common forms of misbehaviour.

Time-Away means encouraging a worked-up child to spend time in a 'Time-Away Space' to calm down on their own, in peace and at their own pace. Time-Away is quite distinct from 'punitive' Time-Out (sitting on the 'naughty step', etc.) and your child should be able to understand this both through the tone of voice you use, and in the way you introduce and describe their Time-Away Space. Indeed, this Time-Away Space should be one that your child enjoys being in (often his or her own room), and once there, your child should be free to self-soothe in the company of his or her own toys etc.

We do not recommend removing a child to a separate room for a 'Time-Away' until they are at least two years of age.

Why this works:

All human beings can get into moments where they have difficulty controlling their emotions and their reactions. This is particularly true of children because they are less able than adults to self-regulate their feelings. One of our key objectives as parents is to help them to learn to control their emotions (see tool **Emotional Resilience**), which is why it is counterproductive for us to 'lose it' and become uncontrollably angry in front of them. Indeed, screaming at children can actually make it much harder for them to calm down because the shock of our outburst causes their whole 'system' to go into alert mode. Instead, we can give our children the opportunity to go to a comforting environment where they will be able to 'self-sooth', calm down and regulate and re-consider their emotion.

Adding the "Uh-oh" at the beginning is a great way to help our children redirect their behaviour. Once they have had an experience of "Uh-oh" followed by 'Time-Away', they will understand that when we say "Uh-oh" it means that they are doing something unacceptable and will need to calm down and change their behaviour. They will also know that if they carry on with the unacceptable behaviour (which should be severe enough to require their separation from the rest of the family), they will be asked to go for Time-Away.

How to use 'Uh-oh' and Time-Away:

1. Once a child breaks an important rule (for e.g. starts hitting someone else), try to be as empathetic as possible (and we know it's hard when your child has 'pushed your buttons'!), and say without anger "Uh-oh" in a positive tone of voice.
2. Follow the "Uh-oh" with an "It seems like you need a bit of Time-Away."

3. Give choices about the process in order to put them in 'thinking mode' rather than 'fighting mode'. For e.g. if they are young enough to be carried "Do you want to walk to your room or shall I carry you?", or if they are older "Do you want to go on your own or shall I come with you?"
   NB: If your child is too old to be carried and does not want to go to their Time-Away space, you need to apply a 'Delayed Consequence' (see tool **Delayed Consequences**) by saying: "It's a shame, I'm going to have to do something about this, but not now", or use the Energy Drain technique (see tool **Energy Drain**).

4. The Time-Away Space should be one that your child enjoys being in (often their own room) and once there, he or she should be free to self-soothe in the company of his or her own toys, books, etc....

5. Once your child is in the 'Time-Away' room, you need to ask: "Do you want the door open or closed?" ...
   This is an essential choice to offer as it makes many children much less anxious about staying in their room. Children will usually say "I want the door open", yet they will often then leave the room the moment you leave the room. At this point you need to say: "Oh, ok you seem to want the door closed?" Then put them back in the room and close the door. They will usually start banging on the door at this point, which means you will need to stay put on the other side of the door to ensure that they won't open the door and that they are safe.
   Once they have stopped their outburst (and only once they have stopped the outburst), leave them there for a few minutes (set a timer if it's helpful). Stay at your post at the door if you're worried that they might do something harmful.

6. When the time is over, ask them: "Are you ready to join us?" Then give them a hug and welcome them back.
   • Try and limit the amount of words that you use after this and DO NOT ask them "Did you understand why I have done this?"

- If your child is older than three, you should ideally follow the Time-Away at a later time with a problem solving session (see tool **Problem Solving**). Make sure this is done a few hours after the Time-Away to ensure that everyone is in a positive emotional state.

NB: Once our children have experienced 'Uh-oh and Time-Away' as a consequence of their actions, we can gently use the word "Uh-oh" to immediately remind them that their behaviour is not acceptable. They will usually redirect their behaviour as soon as they hear you say "Uh-oh", and do so in a spirit of 'self-regulation' rather than fear.

The voice of the Strict parent:

In my older, sterner days 'Time-Out' was my number one punishment and I always applied it with anger, saying something along the lines of: "I cannot believe that you are behaving like this, go to your room immediately!" and I often ended up carrying my children to their rooms myself while they were kicking me. This resulted in lots of punitive time-outs and a poor family connection. Learning how to use "Uh-oh" followed by a 'Time-Away', allows me and my children to take some time off and calm down much faster. It is a real lifesaver as it prevents the typical 'escalations' that everyone usually regrets (particularly because of the real 'disconnection' these escalations lead to).

I seldom have to use Time-Away now because my children tend to immediately and positively redirect their behaviour the moment I say "Uh-oh".

Finally, I must confess that although I know how important it is to say "Uh-oh" in a soft, non-threatening tone, I can still find it hard to erase all signs of anger from my voice. Yet even if my voice or reaction becomes harsher than I'd like, the result is still 100 times better than my old behaviour!

The voice of the All-heart parent:

Although I have seen for myself how effective Uh-oh and Time-Away are, I admit that I still find it challenging to apply because of my fear of losing the connection with my children. When I first used this tool, I was upset by my children's emotional reaction at being separated from me. However, I realised that sending my children to their room in the empathic, step-by-step approach outlined above is far better than trying to calm down a child in a state of uncontrollable rage (as opposed to a tantrum). This is particularly true if my child's misbehaviour is so provocative that I fear 'losing it' myself, or that my other children (and my partner) become drawn into the situation. But I would always recommend that parents explain to their children in advance (when things are going well) what Time-Away is - i.e.: that when things 'heat up', we all need to take some time away in order to calm down and be able to reconnect more positively.

Real life example:

*Our daughter Yasmine (aged four) started teasing our two-year-old daughter Yara, by snatching her things and running away with them. Being unable to chase her and reclaim her possessions, Yara would begin to scream loudly. Although we are both in favour of trusting our children to sort arguments out for themselves (as it teaches them valuable life lessons), Yara was too young to be able to do anything about the situation, except scream. Clearly this situation was affecting the whole family dynamic and so we set a rule during a family meeting (see tool **Family Meetings**) saying "In this house we have a sharing rule, children cannot take their sibling's possessions without their permission."*

So then, when shortly afterwards Yasmine decided to run off with Yara's things again I (Nadim) said, "Uh-oh, it looks like you need some Time-Away".

I then asked her: "Would you like to go by yourself or shall I carry you to your room?" Whereupon she threw herself on the floor and began to have a tantrum and started crying. So I picked her up gently and while I was carrying her, I gave her some empathy by saying: "I can see that this is making you frustrated and sad."

I took her up to her room and then asked, "Would you like the door open or shut". "Open" she screamed back and so I didn't shut her in, but remained in the vicinity to check that she would stay in her room. When I saw her sneaking back out, I said, "Ah, you seem to have decided that you want the door closed?"

But in fact, I didn't need to shut the door because she immediately went back in to her room and stayed there. After a few minutes, I could hear that she had calmed herself down and was now happily playing with her toys. I waited another few minutes (because she needed time to process things) before appearing in the doorway and asking, "Are you ready to come back and join us?" In response, Yasmine held out her arms, gave me a hug and said "Sorry Daddy".

Since then, whenever she shows signs of snatching someone else's things (something that happens far less often) we simply have to say "Uh-oh" and she will immediately hand them back (most of the time!).

⊗ Tool No 26: Delayed Consequences

Use with children aged 3+

Use for: *Replacing empty threats and punishments that you may end up having to retract, all types of misbehaviour, situations where logical consequences cannot be applied, teaching a child the need for boundaries and self-responsibility, learning from mistakes, remedying violent or threatening behaviour.*

This tool can be used on any child who can remember a promise (so usually age three and over).

There are often times when our kids misbehave, and we'd dearly like to teach them a lesson then and there to make sure that they do not repeat this behaviour again. But we are either prevented from acting by circumstance (e.g. we're in the car, or in a hurry), or we are too angry to be empathetic and to find a reasonable, respectful and related consequence (see tool **Logical Consequences**). So, it is a relief to discover that it can actually be more effective to take time to think about the most appropriate consequences and 'announce' it to our children at a later date. This is what we call a 'Delayed Consequence'.

The key is to deliver the Delayed Consequence once the situation has settled, in an empathic, non-punitive way. As with Logical Consequences, Delayed Consequences differ from punishment in that they are delivered with love/empathy and without anger; fit the misbehaviour; focus on the child's poor choice rather than labelling the child itself as 'bad' or 'naughty'; address the present not the past; and are not accompanied by lectures, reminders and guilt trips.

Why this works:

Delayed Consequences work well as they remove the anger and fear - in both parent and child - that come with the act of dealing with misbehaviour 'on the spot'. Delayed consequences encourage our children to be able to *learn* from their behavioural choices, far more successfully than they would have done if faced with conventional punishment given in the 'heat of the moment'. When we move away from the idea of 'blame' or 'shame' and look instead at the cause and effect of our children's poor decision, they cease to feel like the bad guy and are therefore far more willing to learn from their mistake.

How to use Delayed Consequences:

- Imagine that you're in the car and your children start to fight in the back seat, but because you are in a hurry to get somewhere, you are unable to park the car to wait for them to stop. Instead of threatening your children with all sorts of potential punishments, you can use an empathetic statement: "This is a real shame", or "This is so sad" or simply "Ohh…"

- Follow this empathetic statement with: "I'm going to have to do something about this, but not now…"

- Alternatively, if something your child has done 'triggers' you and causes you to feel angry (which makes you more likely to say something that you may later regret), replace an outburst with a declaration: "I'm too angry at the moment to decide what the consequence should be for your misbehaviour, so we'll talk about it when I'm calmer."

- Once the opportunity to illustrate your point arises (it can be up to a week after the event), tell your children something along the lines of: "Remember when you wouldn't stop fighting in the back of the car? Well sadly as a result, I'm not going to be able to take you to the amusement park today." If you deliver the consequence with empathy, without any hint of 'revenge' and without lecturing, relating it as closely as possible to the original misbehaviour, your child will understand that this consequence is a natural and logical one, rather than a punitive punishment.

The voice of the Strict parent:

I can get easily wound up and angered by my children's misbehaviour (particularly when I'm stressed), and my 'gut' reaction is to teach them a harsh lesson that they will remember so that they don't do this again. So I used to say or do things 'in the heat of the moment' that I later regretted, sometimes ending up backtracking on, or 'reducing' punishments (which clearly undermined their effectiveness). What a relief to learn that I didn't always need to do something about my child's misbehaviour immediately, and that I could use Delayed Consequences at later date, once I had calmed down. In fact, Delayed Consequences allowed me to remove myself from some 'highly escalating' situations without feeling that I was giving in or losing control of the situation. It also moved me on from the idea of using immediate punishment, to a place where I could wait until a calmer moment to teach a clear, fair and relevant lesson.

The voice of the All-heart parent:

I didn't like the idea of punishment, but sometimes in extreme situations I found myself being punitive out of frustration and despair. At other times, I wanted the behaviour to stop but couldn't do anything about it (for example while I was driving). So Delayed Consequences came as a great relief, a saviour tool which allowed one to know that something could be done at a later time and without anger, blame and shame.

Real Life Example:

When our daughter Noor was five, she used to love to play with bubble bath. One day I (Nadim) was giving her a bath and thought she'd like the idea of adding some bubble soap so I poured some in the bath without asking her. Noor suddenly started screaming at me at the top of her voice:

"Who said that I wanted bubbles in the bath?! I don't want any bubble bath!"

I was really shocked by this outburst and found myself thinking: "This kind of behaviour needs to be nipped in the bud quickly otherwise it will only get worse as she grows."

But I managed to restrain myself from angrily reprimanding her, remembering that if I shouted back, it would send Noor's brain into 'fight or flight' mode, a place where she wouldn't be able to listen to reason. And besides, how could shouting at her be a logical way of showing her that shouting was not acceptable? I replaced my 'gut' angry reaction with a long "Ohhhhhh..." while at the same time my mind was racing to try and find a 'consequence' that would teach Noor that it is unacceptable to speak like this to her father. But in the heat of the moment, I couldn't find anything suitable that would teach her not to speak like this and that wouldn't run the risk of damaging the connection between us.

So I handed over to Carole (who was thankfully around!) to give myself time to mull over what the best response would be. My 'old style' thinking made me believe that I had to impose a 'strong' consequence, which Noor would remember and learn a lesson from. However, when an opportunity to impose a small consequence the next evening arose, I gave it a go to see if my daughter would understand.

Noor came to me and asked: "Daddy will you play a game with me before dinner?"

I looked her in the eyes and said with empathy: "I'd love to play with you Noor, but when you screamed at me last night I felt so disrespected and sad that I'm afraid it doesn't make me want to play with you now."

I could tell by the way Noor looked that she was thinking about what I'd said. The logic of what I was saying had clearly made sense to her and she seemed to be regretting and reconsidering her behaviour. She walked away sadly.

After dinner (i.e. around one hour later), as Noor was getting prepared for her bath she came to see me and said with a contrite voice: "Daddy, I think it's not a good idea to put any bubble soap in the bath tonight."

And, more to the point, having understood how much she'd hurt me, she never ever screamed at me like that again.

However, as she was close to turning seven, she started back talking. I learnt that this age is appropriately labelled 'the age of rudeness'! Therefore, I thought that the best way to 'curb' this back talking was not to always apply delayed consequences, as other tools such as **'I' Statements**, **Energy Drain** and **Problem Solving**) were more appropriate at that age.

Tool No 27: Energy Drain[37]

> **Use for:** *Replacing threats and punishments, dealing with all types of misbehaviour, sibling squabbles, coping with defiance, teaching children responsibility, balk talk and swearing, bedtimes, mealtimes, mornings and outings.*

Using the term 'Energy Drain' with our children is a 'generic' **Delayed Consequences** technique that can be applied to many problems (for e.g. back talking, sibling squabbles…). The idea is to tell our children that when they misbehave, their behaviour (rather than they, themselves) is giving us an 'Energy Drain'. This enables our children to understand that in order for things to go relatively smoothly, it's best for them not to drain us of energy through their misbehaviour. Using this term also allows for a 'Delayed Consequence', because our children learn that when they drain us of our energy we have little strength left to do things for them later on. Which in turn enables them to understand that only when they work at restoring our energy levels, by doing something helpful for us (for e.g. household tasks), will we be able to 'work' for them again.

Why this works:

What is really powerful about this tool is that it uses a real need (the fact that we 'need' energy to take care of our kids) and makes children realise that their behaviour (rather than themselves) can drain us of this energy. And since this logic is easily understandable for children, it makes this tool very effective. Importantly, it also allows children to learn about their parent's needs and to realise that their actions affect others.

How to use Energy Drain

1. Tell children who are 'playing up' or being uncooperative "This is giving me an energy drain", or "This behaviour is draining me of energy."
2. Follow this up, at a later date (usually a few hours later but can be up to one week after the behaviour occurred) by asking them:

"Since I had an energy drain earlier I'm unfortunately not able to take you to the park right now. How are you planning to recharge my energy so that I will be able to take you?"

- 'Rechargers' could include giving the children house chores (for e.g. wash the floor, dusting, do the dishes, get the leaves from the garden, etc....) or allowing 'time-off for parents' (for e.g. you leave them with a baby sitter or a family member one afternoon so that you can recharge your energy). See tool **Family Contribution**.

The voice of the Strict parent:

When the kids are 'playing up', squabbling or even 'back talking' me, how much more enjoyable (and effective) it is to use the Energy Drain technique, than shouting at them. When I use Energy Drain, it is a pleasure to see my children redirect their behaviour, including asking me how they could help give me back my energy!

The voice of the All-heart parent:

This is one of the tools that I use the most, as it is a very respectful and gentle tool, which delivers a clear message. It doesn't take children long to understand the effect their behaviour has on our energy level. And once they appreciate that our ability to do things for them depends upon our energy levels, they can then understand that it is in their power to restore that energy.

Real life Example:

One day, when our girls were being particularly rowdy and uncooperative, and refusing to listen to our requests we sat them down and told them: "This behaviour is giving us an Energy Drain, we were going to take you to the park for a play, but we are now so tired that we are going to have some quiet time. So instead of going out you will now have to play quietly in your rooms until we are feeling stronger."

The girls were of course disappointed but we could tell that we'd got the message through because next time they were causing chaos they behaved quite differently!

On this next occasion I, Nadim, was in charge of the girls over breakfast, while Carole was having a well-earned rest. The girls soon started creating chaos, bickering loudly and refusing to listen to my attempts to reason with them. So I stood up, went to the door and announced: "Your behaviour is giving me a real Energy Drain. I'm leaving the room now to let you think about how you are going to work at giving me back some of that energy I have lost."

Listening from the other side of the door, I heard the girls go quiet and then, after a while, I heard my eldest say to her sisters "You put the dishes in the dishwasher and I will mop the floor". I was amazed at their reaction! I left them to it and went up to read the newspaper. About twenty-five minutes later they emerged and announced "Dad we wanted you to get your energy back so we've cleared up the kitchen", and indeed they had!

Summary of 'How to effectively deal with 'mis'behaviour'

- Children need boundaries and clear expectations to help them learn to control their impulses.
- When setting a rule, make it non-confrontational by using the third person and keeping it positive.
- Punishment doesn't work as it only teaches kids to act out of fear, or leads them to want to hide things from you.
- Children need to experience the consequence of their decisions, and be made to feel accountable for their actions.
- Children don't need to be made to feel worse in order to do better. To teach them a lesson, you have lots of other options that won't make them feel worse.
- Instead of punishment apply consequences that are reasonable , respectful and related to a 'mis'behaviour.
- Always use empathy when you are imposing a consequence.
- Children will need to take some Time-Away after having done something unacceptable. This often prevents the situation from 'escalating' further.
- Using 'Uh-oh' is a great way to redirect negative behaviour into a more positive one.
- Refrain from issuing 'empty threats' as it undermines your authority.
- Remain consistent in the application of your consequences so that you children understand that you mean what you say.
- You do not have to do something about a 'mis'behaviour immediately: you can often apply **Delayed Consequences**.
- Having an **Energy Drain** is a great way to show children that their actions have consequences on us.

What you should avoid and what you can now choose to do instead:

Avoid:	Replace with:
Issuing Threats and warnings	Setting Rules in the third person and Logical Consequences the *first* time your child breaks the rule
Punishing children and any form of physical abuse	Uh-oh and Time-Away, Logical and Delayed Consequences, Problem Solving (see next chapter)
Naughty-step, Time Out	Uh-oh and Time-Away, Logical and Delayed Consequences
Issuing a consequence while you're very angry	Delayed Consequences

Your notes

Your notes

Coming up in

Chapter 7:

- What a child may be thinking
- Tool No 28: Mistakes as Opportunities for Learning
- Tool No 29: Generating Solutions
- Tool No 30: Problem Solving
- Tool No 31: Family Contribution
- Tool No 32: Family meetings
- Tool No 33: Emotional Resilience
- Summary of 'How to develop your children's self-responsibility and emotional resilience

Chapter 7: How to develop your children's self-responsibility and emotional resilience

Our ultimate goal as parents should be to develop our children's self-responsibility, self-discipline and emotional resilience as these are the key factors that allow our children to stand strong on their own feet.

Self-responsibility is the realisation that we are the author of our choices and actions. Developing self-responsibility means coaching children to find solutions to their own problems, rather than growing up expecting to have their problems solved by others.

A significant part of our role as parents is the ability to let go so that we can teach our children to stand on their own two feet and meet the challenges of adulthood. Once a child is able to use their 'thinking' head to solve their problems, they are well positioned to understand and appreciate their own role in events - including what they are responsible for and what they aren't.

Developing self-discipline requires finding non-punitive solutions to problematic behaviour, and engaging our children in this process rather than focusing on consequences. This is what ensures that problematic behaviour does not (re)occur.

Finally, developing emotional intelligence - the ability to use one's own emotions wisely and to be able to understand how others use theirs - and emotional resilience is a crucial part of a child's evolution through to adulthood. We, as parents, can assist our children's emotional intelligence and resilience by applying the techniques described in this chapter.

What a child may be thinking

My parents are always asking me if I'm ok. I used to tell them if there was something wrong, as they seem to really love finding solutions to my problems. When I share something with them, they always give me a solution for what I should do to feel better or to sort out things with my friends. It's usually pretty helpful but sometimes, I don't really want to do what they suggest - for example if I'm scared of how a friend might react. If I don't follow their advice and they find out, they get cross with me as they say that I don't trust them and that I should listen to them as they have so many years of experience and blah, blah, blah, ...

So now, I try not to talk to them about things where they might suggest things that I don't like doing. And if I do, I just make them think that I'm going to do what they suggest and make them think that everything is all right afterwards.

Tool No 28: Mistakes as Opportunities for Learning

> **Use for:** *Teaching children to learn through experience, learning to 'let go', teaching children to be proactive and responsible, training their 'disappointment muscle', combatting 'entitlement', empowering children.*

We love our children so much that we don't want to see them suffer or be too frustrated, so we often try to protect them from the bad things in life. The irony is that by 'rescuing' our children from difficult situations - often referred to in the literature as Helicopter Parenting, we often steal from them the opportunity to learn the valuable 'trial and error' lessons offered by making mistakes.

Constantly warning children of the 'bad' things that might happen can disempower them, leading them to be less willing to listen to what we have to say. And adding "I told you so", only distances them further from 'owning' their mistake or learning from its 'natural' consequences.

We need to recognise that mistakes suffer from 'inflation', in other words that the cost of mistakes increases as our children grow. For example, if a child falls off his scooter because he was speeding in the park and has a few cuts and grazes as a result, he is more likely to 'appreciate' the danger of speeding. The memory of this earlier mistake will stay with him/her into adulthood and will be one he is likely to recall when he is learning to drive. We call these types of minor mistakes 'affordable' mistakes (as opposed to the 'unaffordable' ones that could involve serious injury or upset).

Similarly, criticising children for making mistakes is not constructive. It can lead them to have lasting feelings of being 'bad or inadequate', and they may become frightened of trying something for fear of failure. It may also cause them to lie in an attempt to hide mistakes from others. So, if parents allow children to make 'affordable' mistakes (within a safe environment of course) their children will see mistakes as opportunities for learning rather than a reason for shame.

Why it works:

Every childhood mistake handled well can become a learning experience, while every childhood mistake handled poorly can become the source of resentment.[38] In other words, letting children make mistakes allows them to understand the 'natural' consequences of these mistakes and be better equipped at preventing them.

Also, children can truly learn the courage to be imperfect when they can laugh and learn from mistakes. It is important not to rescue children from every disappointment, as otherwise they don't have the opportunity to develop their 'disappointment muscles'. We need to "have faith in children that they can survive disappointment and develop a sense of capability in the process."[39]

How to allow children to make mistakes and learn from them:

1. Say what you would do if you were in their shoes, and mention what the 'natural' consequence might be. For e.g.: "If I were you, I would slow down on your scooter because if it goes too fast it may get out of control and you can hurt yourself."

2. If they refuse to listen, then let them make the mistake and allow its 'natural consequence' to occur. In the example above, this means letting them run the risk of falling off their scooter (provided you are in a safe environment and they are not in danger of serious harm).

3. Give empathy (for e.g. "Oh, you hurt yourself!").

4. *DON'T* tell your child: "I told you so", or "If you had listened to me this wouldn't have happened", because to do so makes your warning the focus of the story rather than your child's decision, and the opportunity for learning is therefore lost. Such 'shaming' can also provoke rebellion rather than inspire improvement. Mistakes are only learning opportunities when a child is allowed to take responsibility for them.

5. (Optional): You can tell your child: "You made a mistake. That is fantastic. What can *we* learn from it?" You can use 'we' when

you talk about new learning because many mistakes are made because we haven't taken time for training.

6. (Optional): You can also refer to some mistakes you yourself made, and how you sought to fix them. And you could even invite everyone in the family to share (during dinnertime or during a family meeting) a mistake of the day (or the week) and what they learned from it. The more you respect each other for admitting, solving and remedying your mistakes, the more children will understand that there can be a positive side to getting things wrong.

The voice of the Strict parent:

I tend to be quite controlling and tell my children what they should or shouldn't do. This means that, although I think it can be good for them to experience the consequences of their mistakes, I tend to tell them in advance when I feel they're likely to get hurt, or I force them to wear appropriate clothing before they leave the house. Once the 'mistake' happened, I would remind them that I was right. For example, I would tell them: "You see, I told you that you would get hurt", or "I told you that you would catch a cold!" Now I know that I limit my children's learning experience by saying these things and that it's better to just give them empathy when they are experiencing the natural consequences of their mistake.

The voice of the All-heart parent:

I love my children so much that I find it difficult to see them hurting. I always tried to prevent anything bad from happening to them, as I didn't want to see them 'suffer' or be frustrated. Yet by 'anticipating' issues for them, I was actually preventing them from learning lessons for themselves. One of my most prominent childhood memories is the resentment I felt when my mother constantly warned us of the pitfalls of our actions (followed by lots of 'I told you so's' when we ignored her). I am glad to now able to allow my children to make mistakes in a 'safe' environment, in the knowledge that they will remember these lessons for life.

Real Life Example:

One frosty winter morning when our daughter Noor was five, we told her that she needed to get dressed in preparation for a trip to an outdoor winter fair. When Noor appeared in cotton leggings and socks her Mum, Carole, said: "If I were you I would wear tights and jeans".

Noor returned with a pair of woolly socks, but insisted that the cotton leggings were adequate. Since she seemed adamant on ignoring our advice, we decided that it was time she was allowed her to make an 'affordable mistake' so that she could learn from the consequences. And so we didn't force her to change, nor did we take extra layers 'just in case'. After a few hours at the fair, sliding down cold slides and standing out in the frosty weather, Noor began to feel frozen and tearful. But instead of saying "I told you so", we used our empathy tools, giving her a big hug and telling her how sorry we felt for her. The next morning, she came downstairs and proudly announced that she had been careful to put on multiple layers to combat the cold. And from then on she was careful to check the weather outside before getting dressed. She is clearly taking pride in feeling responsible for her own well-being, a form of self-empowerment unlikely to have happened at her age had she not been allowed to make a mistake.

Tool No 29: Generating Solutions

> **Use with children aged 3+**
>
> **Use for:** *Empowering children, letting them find solutions to their problems, fostering self-responsibility and independence, social problems.*

This tool usually follows a session of 'active listening' (see tool **Active Listening**). Having actively and reflectively listened to our children's problems, we then encourage them to take responsibility for working the problem out. For example, once our child has shared with us that they have no friends at school and we have 'actively' listened to what they have to say, we can then ask in an empathetic way: "What could you do about this?", followed by "Do you want to hear what other children have tried?"

In order to generate the right solutions and problem solve efficiently, we have to recognise *who* has the problem and *what* they can do about it.

It is important to know that there are two kinds of problems/ challenges that our children can encounter. The first is the kind of problem that our children are themselves experiencing, for example struggling with their homework.

This type of problem is not helped by our attempting to take it on ourselves and try to solve it for our children, including doing their homework for them. Whereas encouraging them to try to independently find solutions to their problem will make them much more likely to try to finish the task.

The second type is the problem that we, the *parents* are experiencing, e.g. our children are being rude to *us*. To learn how to solve the problems that *you* are experiencing with your child refer to the tool **Problem Solving**.

Why this works:

Coaching our children to generate solutions to their own problems (rather than give them solutions ourselves) gives them much more incentive to be pro-active and independent. When they are able to identify a solution to their problem and then solve the issue for themselves, they will feel both empowered to carry out the solution that they choose and will also feel pleased with themselves. So much more effective in the long run than assuming that their parents will always be there to solve problems for them!

How to use Generating Solutions:

1. Place ownership of the problem on the child's shoulders by asking:
    1. "What could you do about it?" (for issues that might need a resolution in the future).
    2. Or "Sounds like you're not happy with what happened? What could you do differently next time?" (for issues that have already taken place).
2. The answer is usually: "I don't know", particularly when the child hasn't been coached at finding solutions to their own problems previously.
3. Say: "Do you want to know what some other kids have tried?" or "Do you want some ideas?"
    - If child says "No", say "If you change your mind, I'm here to listen."
    - If child says "Yes", give them a 'menu' of possible solutions. You should give them at least two possible solutions. As children (particularly younger ones), will tend to choose the first solution that you suggest, we would recommend starting with an idea that your child is unlikely to choose.
    - After each solution, ask your child: "How would that work for you?"If you don't have ideas 'on the spot', it is ok to tell your child, "Let me have a think about it and check what other kids have tried and I'll get back to you".
4. Once your child has chosen one of the solutions that you offered, or comes up with their own solution say to them, "Let me know how this works out, good luck!"
    If they haven't been 'inspired' by any of the solutions, you can always leave them to come up with the solution at a later date. The

important thing is that they recognise that you are supporting them as well as encouraging them to think for themselves, both now and in the future.

The voice of the Strict parent:

I am a 'solution finder' and I used to think that I needed to share my 'wisdom' with my kids, giving them solutions as soon as they started sharing a problem with me. Then, I discovered the importance of letting children think for themselves, which means that I now focus on actively listening first and then encouraging them to find solutions for themselves. Yes, it can be a tricky tool to master, but I can tell you from the amazing results I've seen that it's really worth the effort.

The voice of the All-heart parent:

I had little awareness as to how many times I was rushing in with parental reassurances and 'make it better' solutions. Being naturally protective, it is quite challenging for me to encourage a child to 'own' their own problem, yet I can see that when I do, they feel so much more motivated to find a solution and feel proud for having done so. This is a great tool to boost everyone's self-esteem.

Real life Example:

Our seven-year-old Noor, was falling behind on her reading, yet was remaining resistant to the instruction from both us, and her teacher, that she should practise her reading for half an hour a day. At first, I (Carole) took charge of the reading duties, but I was not being consistent and sometimes felt unable to 'force' my daughter to stick to the daily practice. This made Nadim, the stricter parent, stressed about the inconsistency of the 'practice makes perfect message'. So, he went to the opposite extreme and tried to enforce a strict reading schedule. This seemed to worsen the problem, causing Noor to become distressed and less motivated to read.

It was at this point that we realised we were making the mistake of confusing Noor's problem with our problem, which meant that we were transferring our anxieties on to her. We realised that the answer was to encourage her to take responsibility for her own reading issues. The best way to do this was to motivate and empower Noor by encouraging her to find solutions to her 'mental block' with the help of our Generating Solutions tool. And so we sat down with Noor and began by asking her to think about why it is so important that she should learn to read properly.

"I need to be able to read signs and instructions and things like that", she responded.

"So what is the best way to improve your reading?" we asked.

"Practice", Noor answered.

"Great, so you understand why you need to practice, but you seem to be struggling to actually do it, so what do you think you should do to help yourself?"

"I don't know", she answered (a typical initial response for kids of her age).

"Do you want to know what other kids have done to get themselves reading?" we asked her and when she nodded, we started generating solutions with her.

We offered her the first possible solution: "Well, some children have approached their reading practice with a positive attitude, and as soon as they discovered how fascinating it is to discover new stories, they started reading all day long".

Noor wasn't too sure what to think of this and ended up answering: "Uh, not sure that would work for me as I find it hard to read."

We then offered another solution: "Some children, knowing that they have to read for half an hour a day, like to be in charge of exactly when this half an hour happens. Do you have a preference for when you'd like to do your half an hour reading?"

To which she answered: "Yes, I'd like to do it in the morning before you wake up."

This surprised us a lot because she'd always seemed to refuse to read if we weren't next to her all the time. Yet sure enough, the next morning she arrived in our room, announcing proudly that she had just spent the last half hour reading her book. She then explained to us what she had read *and showed us the words she had been struggling with. The next day she skipped the morning reading session, as we had to leave early for an outing. But come the evening, when we mentioned that her reading practice had yet to be done, she sat down, opened her book and read to us and then her sisters without the signs of stress that she had previously experienced. And better was to come for the following morning she arrived in our room and said "Guess what Dad? I'm really proud of myself because I read the whole book on my own this morning!" Her lesson in Generating Solutions had allowed her to 'own' her problem, replacing the stress of feeling obliged to fulfil a duty for other's benefit, with the far more rewarding sense of personal empowerment and achievement. A great life lesson with far reaching implications.*

Tool No 30: Problem Solving

Use with children aged 3+

Use for: *Handling effectively all types of misbehaviour, encouraging your child's self-responsibility, solving sibling squabbles, winning your child's cooperation, solving social and school problems.*

This is an effective tool to solve all types of misbehaviour and is a great replacement for **Logical Consequences** (see corresponding tool), particularly when our children are four years and older.

Indeed, it is always better for us to use 'positive discipline', i.e. focusing on problem solving to find solutions as a means of changing unacceptable behaviour, rather than depend upon consequences - because it makes our children more responsible (and not just accountable) for their actions.

When we have a problem with our children's behaviour, we first need to identify and define it by explaining how it has affected us by using **'I feel' messages** (see corresponding tool). We can then work with our children to find a solution that works for everyone concerned and prevents the problem from reoccurring.

In order to understand how we can problem solve, we need to recognise that there are two types of problem. The first kind is the problem that our children are experiencing themselves, for example they are struggling with their homework or they feel that they have no friends. The second type is the problem that we, the parent are experiencing, e.g. our child is being rude to us. In order to problem solve efficiently one needs to recognise *who* has the problem and *what* they can do about it.

The following tool refers to solving a problem that we as a parent 'own'. In other words, the problem is one that has been created by the child and is now creating difficulties for us: e.g. our child is lying to us, or is stealing, or any other unacceptable behaviour.

It is important to use this tool a few hours after a problem has arisen, since when a child is (or you yourself are) still 'triggered' by an event, any suggestion that they change their approach can lead them to become defensive and unwilling to generate solutions or hear suggestions.

As a Problem Solving session occurs a few hours after the event, you may wish to use other tools prior to using this one, such as applying a logical consequence (see **Logical Consequences**), or a Time-Away (see **Uh-oh and Time-Away**).

Why this works:

This tool allows us to focus on solutions instead of consequences or punishment. Children can participate in setting up rules, choosing appropriate consequences and selecting the way that they prefer to be reminded should a misbehaviour occur. This teaches children to be responsible and is therefore far more effective than any other form of discipline. This is the true path to self-responsibility.

How to use Problem Solving:

1. Initiate the problem solving by doing something your child likes, e.g. playing a game of cards, or introduce it during a family meeting (see tool **Family Meetings**).
2. Identify and define the issue (using an **'I feel' Messages**) e.g. "When you spoke to me the way you did, I felt disrespected and I felt hurt." Always keep the sentence in the present tense so that our children feel that we are addressing a specific issue in the here and now, rather than 'amalgamating' past issues.
3. Generate possible alternative solutions *together,* focusing on what you and your child could do differently. Let your children come up with solutions if they are old enough (4+) and then add your suggestions.
4. Evaluate the alternative solutions and after each option, ask: "How would that work for you?"
5. Decide on the best solution(s) *together* and work out ways of implementing it.

6. Ask your children: "If you forget our agreement and start behaving in the 'old' way, how would you like to be reminded of your new resolution?" Help them come up with a fun way (which would work for both of you) to help them 'reconnect' with their commitment. For e.g. you can agree to clap your hands twice or sing a song when they do the behaviour again (see example below).

7. Optional (if you have time and your child is older than five): Make your children responsible for deciding their own consequences. Finish your problem solving session by discussing what the logical consequence should be if your child decides not to follow your agreement. For example, you could tell them: "You've agreed to do this and I am sure you will, but just in case you started to misbehave in this way again, even after I'd reminded you of our agreement, what do you think the consequences should be?" Encourage your child to suggest possible consequences and decide together on the best one to be used from now on.

NB: The first time you ask your children to suggest their own consequence, they may be too surprised to come up with any suggestions, in which case you should offer your own. You could start by offering a 'strong' consequence, one that might sound more akin to a punishment, which will make your other suggestions seem milder (and more desirable by comparison!). Once your children have done a couple of these problem solving sessions with you, you'll be amazed at how reasonable they can be in suggesting fair consequences for themselves.

The voice of the Strict parent:

I had a certain resistance to this tool because I was sceptical about using 'democratic' approaches, like involving children in finding solutions to their issues. Far better, I mistakenly thought, to teach through 'appropriate' consequences. I also believed that my children, who were three and five when I discovered this tool, were far too young to be able to offer reasonable solutions. However, once I tried the tool, I saw how much I had undervalued my children's ability to be able to understand how to solve their own problems. Once I'd allowed and encouraged them to participate in finding solutions, I saw how quickly their behaviour and attitude can change.

The voice of the All-heart parent:

I just love problem solving as it is an amazing replacement to using consequences (which I never feel totally comfortable with because of the strong emotional reaction experiencing a 'consequence' can have on a child). It is a great tool to use with any child aged three or more because of the way it makes them feel much more self-disciplined and responsible. I would also recommend that you never forget the last step, i.e. "How would you like to be reminded?" (See example below.) As a quick jog of the memory is often what is needed to encourage children to redirect when they begin reverting back to an old 'mis'behavioural habit.

Real life Example:

*Recently, we were going through the agenda of our weekly family meeting (see **Family Meetings**) and it came to four-year-old Yasmine's turn to raise the issues/needs she'd wanted to bring to the meeting.*

"Well Dad, when you shout, it scares me so I want you to shout less", she said.

I (Nadim) was quite amazed at my daughter bringing this up during our family meeting as I was already making a big effort to shout less. I was just about to defend myself and tell her that she just had to accept the way I was, but then I suddenly realised that it was important for her to know that her needs were important too, so I replied instead: "I'd like that too."

"Good", Yasmine said back, and followed with: "So what are you going to do about it?"

"Well I commit to try very hard not to shout so much", I replied. "But, I'd also like some help from you so that I can stop myself before the shouting

begins, can you give me any ideas as to how I can do this?"

At this point Noor, Yasmine's six-year-old sister chipped in "Well either you could take Time-Away or you could turn to the wall and make your angry face so that we don't have to see it."

"Thanks for the great ideas!" I smiled.

"Any time!" she replied.

"There's another way you can help" I added "The fact is that the majority of times I find myself raising my voice is when we are in a hurry and you aren't getting a move on. So what can we do to make sure that this doesn't happen? How can I remind both of you to hurry up without shouting?"

Noor and Yasmine thought about this awhile and started having a giggle about all the different things I could say to them to make them get ready faster. They ended up agreeing on: "How about, rather than screaming, you sing to us 'Let's all go, let's all go' to the tune of Frozen's 'Let it go'?"

And that's what happened and it works wonders because the girls find it a fun way to be 'motivated' (instead of constant reminders!) ... and way better than having to encounter 'shouty' Dad.

✖ Tool No 31: Family Contribution

> **Use for:** *Building self-esteem and self-evaluation, developing responsibility and empathy, encouraging intrinsic motivation, building core values, developing motor skills and abstract learning, offering feedback, learning through mistakes, encouraging your child to try new things, developing empathy.*

As parents, we need to enable our children to understand and practice 'self-responsibility' so that they are able to cope with real life challenges. One of the best ways to increase children's self-responsibility, as well as their sense of purpose and belonging is to make them participate in day-to-day household tasks. As we explained in the introduction, when children feel a stronger sense of belonging and significance, it substantially reduces their inclination to misbehave.

When young children are encouraged to practice, under supervision, some of life's basic 'survival' skills (such as tidying up, cleaning, cooking, etc.) they learn many useful lessons along the way. However, it is important that they are allowed to make (safe) mistakes as they are learning, because the lessons they will learn from these 'trials and errors' are much more valuable than any lessons they are 'told'. So tempting as it is to rush into help or take over from your children when they are doing something less than perfectly, try to give them a bit of time to work it out for themselves. (See **Mistakes as Opportunities for Learning.**)

Giving children 'duties' (and making them fun wherever possible), is also an important way to foster in your children a sense of family (as well as social) involvement. 'Helping out' tasks when performed routinely, also discourages even the youngest of children from assuming that they are 'entitled' to get anything they want. Moreover, a number of studies have shown that children who become accustomed to doing family chores from an early age are far more likely to be successful in adulthood[40].

However, it is vital that children learn to be 'helpers' for the intrinsic motivation of having a useful role rather than for the promise of a reward. If for example, children get used to being paid for housework, the payment rather than the satisfaction of helping out and contributing to the family, will become the motivator.

Offering money for doing chores can also create the expectation in children that everything they do should be rewarded. This sense of entitlement can hinder their development later on, when they discover that they must fulfil many adult responsibilities that don't offer any immediate reward and simply have to be done as part of daily life.

Research shows that the external motivation provided by the reward becomes stronger than the internal motivation of contributing to family life or of simply doing good[41]. We therefore generally advise against using rewards to motivate children towards contributing to family life or improving their behaviour. Look to other tools in this Toolbox for far more effective ways of encouraging cooperation and motivating your child.

Why this works:

When children understand the importance of looking after other's needs, as well as their own, they are receiving an invaluable guide to how to interact with the real world, both now and in the future. Not only will regular household tasks/chores increase a child's competence, but it will also help them feel in control of their own actions and increase their ability to make the right decisions. And most important of all, contributing to family life gives children what they most crave - significance and a sense of purpose. In other words, once you can involve your children in being useful family members they are far less likely to try to gain your attention through misbehaviour.

How to use Family Contribution:

At an early age – (we often call the below four steps to self-responsibility):

1. Give your child a task that is age appropriate (for e.g. ask an 18-month-old to pour their own juice). Make sure that you teach them how to do it properly, since us adults often make

the mistake of expecting children to accomplish tasks that they haven't been trained in.

2. Allow them to make a mistake and experience the 'natural' consequences using observation rather than reprimand (for e.g. let your child discover that pouring with one hand will usually lead water/juice to spill).

3. Help them understand how they could 'improve' the way they do this task next time. And if they are old enough, ask them for suggestions as to how they think the task could be done differently.

4. Give them the opportunity of doing the task again so that they get a chance to do it 'right'.

When your child(ren) are five years and older:

- Use a family meeting (see Family Meetings) to discuss the importance of everyone helping out.
- Make a list of chores, focusing first on detailing the household tasks that you and your partner already perform (for example, driving children to school, shopping, cleaning, etc.). Giving your children examples of the significant time and labour that parents contribute to the family will significantly reduce your child's resistance to doing their own part of the chores.
- Then ask your children for ideas as to what chores they could do (for e.g. making their beds, setting the table, cleaning the table, watering the plants, taking the rubbish out, etc....)
- Have them agree on who will do what.
- If they start arguing about who does what, tell them not to worry, as they will be able to swap or change their chores the following week.
- Try to make the tasks fun rather than a 'chore' or something to be 'got through'.
- Ensure that the tasks are worked into a routine so that they become habitual.

The voice of the Strict parent:

I used to believe that allowing my children to participate in the running of the home was a good way of messing up our efficient routine. I am a perfectionist and rather impatient so I find it difficult not to intervene, for example when I see my child accidentally tipping food off her plate as she takes it over to the sink. I had to learn to put my children's need (to develop their skills through trial and error) before my own need (not to have to clear up their mess). Changing my attitude allowed me to realise how important it is for them to play a part in family life, master a new skill and feel all the prouder for it.

The voice of the All-heart parent:

I used to run a Montessori nursery so I know how important it is to encourage children to participate in 'practical life', and to learn responsibility from an early age. Yet once I became a Mum, it was all too easy to think, "I'm in a rush so I will make their beds or lay the table for them today." And I still have to often remind myself not to do the many things for my children that they are capable of doing for themselves, even when they ask me. The fact is that the more opportunity we give them to participate, and do things for themselves, the more they will willingly join in, and feel proud of the part that they are playing.

Real life example:

Carole's Montessori training showed us the importance of getting our children to participate and be involved in family life from an early age. So for example, from the age of 18 months our children learnt to carry their own plates from the table and to clean up any spills, from the age of two they were able to lay the table themselves and from three they could make their bed, clear away the dishes, clean down the surfaces, etc. We also encouraged them to divide these chores between them, which helped them learn the art of cooperation and working together.

And we also introduced the idea of doing family tasks together, like washing the car. The other day, after we had all worked hard together washing the car, my daughter Noor came up to me (Nadim), and said "Daddy thanks for all your help with the car!"

I replied "And thank you too Noor!"

To which she replied "Yeah Dad, but you did more work on the car than the rest of us!"

It really struck me how well she had understood the idea of teamwork, and how each person shares equally the responsibility for doing the task according to their own abilities.

Tool No 32: Family meetings[42]

> **Use with children aged 4+**
>
> **Use for:** *Building connection with your child and the rest of the family, learning cooperation, teaching by example, solving problems, participation, value setting, fostering empathy and understanding, learning to express one's own needs, increasing family harmony.*

Family meetings are an invaluable tool for family (re)connection and for encouraging our children to cooperate. These regular get-togethers (usually weekly) make every family member feel that their 'needs' are important and are a great setting to teach good values. Family meetings encourage children to be involved in the decision-making side of family life, as well as teaching them to take responsibility for setting their own rules, including deciding the consequences of breaking these rules.

Family meetings should ideally include the whole family so make sure you invite even the youngest of siblings to join you, giving them an activity, such as drawing if they are too little to participate in the discussion side of things. The benefits of sitting down together and discussing how the family should work together are enormous. Most of all, a family meeting allows our children to feel a sense of belonging and responsibility at being 'in touch' with other family members.

Why this works:

Family meetings create a great opportunity for each family member to communicate and express their needs, and to help find solutions to both their own problems and the rest of the family's. These meetings create a real sense of family unity and teach children invaluable life skills such as showing gratitude, appreciating others, expressing one's needs, sharing responsibilities and solving problems. Most importantly, everyone is given an opportunity to be heard by all, which is invaluable.

How to do Family Meetings (see example below)

- Aim for a family meeting once a week.
- Choose a Chair person and Secretary.
- Start with compliments and gratitude at the beginning of the meeting: each person taking turns at addressing every family member to express gratitude and/or a compliment. For e.g. our five-year-old daughter once told our three-year-old daughter who was going through a 'biting phase': "Thank you for not biting me this week"!
- Go through the 'Agenda' (see example below to clarify some of these points).
  1. Individual issues: each family member raises their need or problem.
  2. Discussion or Problem Solving of the individual issues: i.e. brainstorming solutions to family issues (see tool **Problem Solving**).
  3. Discussion and allocation of daily and weekly household tasks/chores (see tool **Family Contribution**).
  4. Planning Activities and family fun.
  5. If you have time, play a game together.
  6. End with a family hug!

The voice of the Strict parent:

It was not in my nature to use lots of positivity as a parenting technique, and since family meetings start with gratitude and compliments to each family member, they turned out to be a bit more challenging than expected. But I had to admit that opening the meeting with a round of compliments and gratitude sets the scene for addressing the needs and 'challenges' of the family in a really effective, caring and sharing way. I find these meetings particularly useful for sorting out sibling issues, and for making my children responsible for setting rules and consequences that they agree with. Indeed, I am constantly amazed at how responsible my children can be when I give them the opportunity to be.

The voice of the All-heart parent:

When I discovered family meetings, it was immediately clear that they were a great way for us to reconnect as a family and to be able to express our needs freely without blame or shame. However, given my tendency to be a bit disorganised, our weekly meetings would often slip. I didn't make a big deal out of it, as our family dynamics was already becoming really positive thanks to our other tools. But there was no doubt that when we missed a family meeting, the family became less connected as the children began to forget their responsibilities and became more challenging. I now make a real effort to keep these weekly appointments. I find them particularly invaluable before a holiday or other potentially stressful event, as the meetings give us the space to anticipate and agree on important issues in advance.

Real Life Example:

Kathy wanted to build a connection with her two sons Mark, aged nine, and Henry, aged six, so she decides to instigate a family meeting every Friday evening after dinner. She explained to her boys that from now on they will be having a weekly meeting together and what this 'get together' will involve. And that its purpose is to allow each of them to raise any 'worries, concerns or needs' that they might have, so that the rest of the family can try and offer help and support. She added, that it will be special family time together, rather than a 'chore' and will end in a nice ritual like a meal, a film or a game.

"I am going to put a sheet of paper on the fridge door and I want you to write down any problem that you'd like us to help you with, and we will address it together at the Friday meeting."

"Err...ok" Mark says. But Henry is more enthusiastic and rushes to write down,

"I'd like to go on more adventures!"

After a while Mark adds, "My friends get more play dates than I do, that's not fair!"

Then her husband Ed chips in, "I'd like a bit of help with gardening the vegetable patch."

Kathy adds her request, "And I'd like to be allowed a lie in until 8am on Saturdays."

With their needs written down, Kathy calls the children to the meeting at the agreed time.

Henry decides that he is going to be the 'chair' and make sure everyone follows the agenda and that the points raised are recorded. Kathy then explains:

"Ok we kick off each meeting with everyone either complimenting or showing gratitude to the rest of the family in turn. So I'd like to start by telling Mark how proud I am of the effort he has been making with his homework. And Henry, I am really impressed by how helpful you have been this week around the house. And Ed, thank you for trying to grow vegetables for the family!"

The boys and their Dad then follow in turn, each showing appreciation for each other.

Each family member then raises their issue.

"Says here that you want more adventures", says Kathy "Do you know what kind of adventure you would like? We've been to most of the places on your wish list!"

"Hmm" says Henry thinking hard and then in a light bulb moment says "I know! Why don't you take us on a magical mystery adventure, the kind where I don't know where we are going until we get there!" says Henry.

"It's a deal Henry! Dad and I will keep it top secret. How about next Saturday?" says Kathy.

"What about me having more friends come to visit?" says Mark.

"Well, that's a bit tricky at the moment because you only have one afternoon at home a week, but maybe there's a compromise?" Kathy says.

"I know!" says Mark. "How about on the days I can have friends over, I invite like three at a time, that way I get to see a whole bunch of them… and they might invite me back to theirs on another day, so I don't have to go to after school club." "Great idea", says Ed, pleased to hear his son finding a solution to his own needs.

And the rest of the meeting proceeds in the same fashion, the boys agree to Kathy's request for a bit of morning 'me' time and everyone suggests a vegetable they would like to take care of in Ed's vegetable patch.

"Right, any objections to the meeting ending with a game of hearts and a bowl of ice cream?" Ed suggests, but the boys have already rushed off to find the cards, bowls and spoons.

Tool No 33: Emotional Resilience

> ***Use for:*** *helping your child sooth themselves and 'self-regulate', encouraging your child to take responsibility, teaching self-control, coping with frustration and disappointments, and helping your child deal with bullying and rejection.*

Resilience is the quality of being able to persevere and adapt when things go awry. It is a key part of our success in school, at work and our satisfaction in life, because it enables us to better cope with life's adversities and setbacks. A lack of resilience can make life feel and appear much harder than it really is and affect our physical health, our mental health and the quality of our relationships.

The key to increasing resilience is about changing the way we *think* about adversity[1].

The tools presented in this book will help your children achieve a higher level of resilience, as they help them to understand that *their choices* and their beliefs will ultimately determine the level of satisfaction they feel in their lives.

We will focus here on the importance of boosting Emotional Resilience and self-control.

Emotional Resilience is about experiencing feelings and knowing how to grow stronger from them, rather than remaining 'stuck in them'. When children show us their emotions, they are giving us an opportunity to relate to their feelings, and to 'coach them' through the emotional 'roller coasters' that they experience during their childhood. We need to help them understand that their feelings are not the problem, but that sometimes their 'mis'behaviour is[2], and that there are ways to remedy it.

The way to achieve this is by showing them empathy in every situation, even if we do not agree with their display of emotion, or their behaviour. Rather than reinforcing their behaviour, showing them empathy encourages them to reconnect with us, thereby allowing us to 'redirect' them to a more positive behaviour (see tool **Empathy and Validation**).

Once children feel secure in their emotional experiences they will be able to trust their feelings, take responsibility for them and understand the effect that they have on others. This early emotion training provides the key to raising children's emotional intelligence and nurtures resilience, so that they are better equipped to deal with life's challenges such as bullying and rejection.

Children also need to learn to be patient and to train their 'disappointment muscle' (see tool **Mistakes as Opportunities for Learning**). When they learn how to cope with frustrating and emotionally distressing situations, they acquire the ability to 'self-regulate'[3] and to sooth themselves out of their upset.

Finally, it's important to note that emotional resilience often starts with the parent working on their ability to acknowledge and gain control over their own emotional state, both as individuals and as a parenting couple.

Why this works:

Emotional resilience is one of the cornerstones to achieving a successful and happy life, and it is significantly shaped during childhood. Research shows that the ability to increase self-control and to delay gratification is critical to living a successful and fulfilling life[4]. Children constantly learn from us, which is why we should use our status as guides to teach and motivate them to 'self-regulate' their own emotional state, and understand its impact on others.

How to increase your child's Emotional Resilience:

1. Developing Patience

The first step to increasing children's resilience is to teach them patience and how to cope with frustration, as these are essential life skills that children must learn from as early an age as possible. Here are a few simple examples of how you can teach your child to be more patient:
- Find opportunities for them to 'practise' waiting. For example, when kids want to talk to you and you're having a conversation

with someone else, instead of letting them interrupt you, ask them to put their hand on top of yours, and you can put your hand on top of theirs to show them that you're aware that they want to speak with you. Once you've finished your conversation, make sure that you address them, and try and give them undivided attention - time permitting, so that you reward their patience.

- Do not 'reward' screaming or impatient behaviour by giving in to these types of behaviours. When kids want something, teach them to wait for it, and if they whine, they won't get it this time and will have to wait until next time. See tool **Being Consistent**.

- Model waiting yourself. There are many opportunities in everyday life where you can show your children that you need to wait for things that you really want. Show them tactics to distract their attention from something that they really want by focusing on something else. This has proved to be one of the most efficient tactics to enable the delaying of gratification[5].

- Teach them to play by themselves: for e.g. don't interrupt your child if they are playing alone happily, so they get used to having more autonomy (see tool **Playing**).

2. Dealing with bullying and hurtful words

- When your child shares experiences from school or other settings where they seem to have experienced some form of bullying or rejection, it is essential to listen actively and acknowledge their pain, hurt and frustration (See tool **Active Listening**), This will make them feel heard, supported and understood.

- Teach them that children who bully are usually hurting, angry and lonely, are probably being bullied at home, and may not realise that being hurtful is wrong.

- More importantly, they need to learn how to stand up for themselves by being assertive and letting the 'bully' know that their behaviour is not ok.

- Using the tool **Generating Solutions**, make sure that your child 'owns' the problem, but you can suggest ideas of what 'other children have tried' to cope with similar situations in a problem solving session. Here are some ideas of assertive language that children have used to good effect to answer someone who has used hurtful words:
  - "Thank you for sharing"
  - "That's your opinion and you can keep it"
  - "Really? Thanks"
  - "Are you having a bad day?"

  NB: This by no means covers all aspects of bullying. These are just a few examples to illustrate how we can coach our children to deal with some instances of rejection and bullying.

3. Emotion Coaching

Most of the tools in this Toolbox are designed to boost children's emotional resilience and teach them the importance of self-control by coaching them to master their emotions. Here are examples of how you can use some of the tools to this effect:

- **Modelling**: Teach your child to better manage their emotions by demonstrating to them instances where you manage your own emotions.
- **Empathy and Validation**: Let your child know that you care about what they are going through when they are experiencing an emotion, be it a positive one (excitement or joy) or a negative one (anger, frustration).
- **Active Listening**: Allow your child to share their problems and emotions without feeling judged. And let them process their feelings rather than immediately giving them solutions.
- **Positive Redirection**: Redirect your child's attention to something more positive, in order to prevent the strong emotions that can occur when they hear us saying "No" too often.

- **<u>Mistakes as Opportunities for Learning</u>**: Encourage them to learn from their own experiences by allowing them to make 'affordable' mistakes, and by training their 'disappointment muscle'.
- **<u>'I feel' Messages</u>**: Encourage your child to understand that their behaviour has an effect on other people's emotions by expressing your own feelings with an 'I feel' message.
- **<u>Rewind and Replay</u>** and **<u>Repair</u>**: Allow them to understand the importance of humility and forgiveness by displaying it towards them.
- **<u>Diffusing Whining and Arguing</u>**: Teach your child to get used to the frustrating fact that they cannot always get what they want. And model to them that you are able to manage your own emotions, even when they provoke you.
- **<u>Problem Solving</u>** and **<u>Generating Solutions</u>**: Allow your child to take responsibility for their actions and find solutions to life's challenges. And when they give suggestions, ask them how these solutions might (or might not) benefit others as well.
- **<u>Family Meeting</u>**: Encourage yourself and the rest of the family to share stories and find solutions to different types of problems.

The voice of the Strict parent:

Understanding the extent to which we need to coach our children emotionally and the ways in which this can be used to teach self-control and boost resilience in my children, has probably been the biggest and steepest learning experience for me in my parenting journey. It was difficult to admit the extent of both the short term and longer-term impact that my reactions can have on my children, and their longer-term beliefs about life. I realised how important it is for me to give them empathy, and to enable them to come out of their emotional distress much faster by managing my own reactions to their behaviour. I still have to remind myself to do this on a daily basis as it is still sometimes difficult when I am stressed by other things. But with a good dose of awareness and this comprehensive Toolbox, it has certainly been a lot easier.

The voice of the All-heart parent:

I am more of a 'feeler' than a 'thinker', and have always encouraged my children to express their feelings freely and as often as they could. However, I hadn't realised how much I had to learn about coaching my children emotionally to truly foster my children's emotional intelligence and increase their resilience. The years I have spent studying the most effective parenting strategies and turning them into tools have actually helped me understand a great deal about myself, and my own emotional history. I realised that the reason why I can find it difficult to 'recover' from some of my emotional states is because my own parents used to 'minimise' my feelings with statements like "It's not that bad", believing they were reassuring me. With this new self-awareness, I now make sure that I do not discount my children's feelings and instead find constructive ways for them to grow through their emotions and learn to respond with assertiveness to rejection and bullying; something I never learned as a child. I also make sure that my children are getting used to experiencing some disappointments and frustrations, to help them learn self-control and become better at self-soothing and self-regulating.

Real Life Example:

Our 5-year-old daughter Yasmine, went through a phase of feeling rather easily put down and affected by other people's comments, especially her eldest sister's. So during One-on-one Time, we talked about this and she shared how she hates it if someone tells her something nasty. So I used the tool **_Generating Solutions_** *and gave her some ideas of the positive attitude that other girls have taken when experiencing hurtful comments, with examples of statements such as 'Thank you for sharing' or 'That is your opinion'.*

A few days later day, her older sister who was going through a phase of saying anything that goes through her mind and enjoying provoking reactions in others, tells Yasmine 'you are not invited to David's birthday, he doesn't like you anymore'. Yasmine nearly broke into tears, but seemed to remember our conversation at the last minute, as she looked at her sister assertively and responded with "Thank you for sharing this information, it's your opinion".

She had actually used both ideas I had given her in her response and I thought 'good for you'!

Summary of 'How to develop your children's self-responsibility and emotional resilience

- Children need to train their 'disappointment muscles' early on so that they can become more resilient and realistic in their expectations.
- As mistakes suffer from 'inflation', allow your children to make as many (affordable) mistakes as possible while they are young. They will learn far more from their own mistakes than from anything that you tell them.
- Children are much more likely to feel empowered if they come up with their own solution to a problem. You can coach them to do this using **Generating Solutions**.
- Instead of focusing on consequences, it is much better to focus on finding solutions to issues and challenges by involving your children in the decision-making process.
- Use **Problem Solving** from the age of three to solve almost any behavioural (and other) issues, and to encourage your children to become responsible for their own actions.
- One of your primary roles is to support your children in their willingness to do 'the right thing', so remember to always ask them how they would like to be reminded of the decisions that they make during a 'problem solving' session.
- **Family Contribution** and chores are a very important part of creating better family dynamics and preventing our children from feeling 'entitled'.
- **Family Meetings** are one of the most important tools that you can implement to improve family dynamics and increase your children's self-responsibility and self-discipline.
- Teach your children patience and how to cope with frustration as these are essential life skills.
- To boost your children's resilience, show them that *they have the choice of their experience*, and that they can find solutions to recover from their emotional distress.

Your notes

Conclusion

Parents of grown-up children say that when they look back, they don't know where their kids' childhood went; it just flew by. They also say they wished they'd been able to enjoy their children more at the time. We sincerely hope that this book and its parenting toolbox will help you enjoy your journey as a parent and as a family, while you are well and truly in the thick of it, so that you don't look back with regret.

As parents we can only do the best we can, make ourselves aware of how we parent and trust that if we do give it our 'best shot', that our kids will turn out to be well-adjusted, self-responsible, decent and happy human beings.

This guide should build on the insights that you already have. The techniques and tools that we shared should serve as a 'framework' that you can use to help you deal with most situations, and to help your children stand strong on their own. Our ultimate objective is that you use this book to balance firmness and consistency with a generous measure of hopefulness and joy, so that you can help your whole family to work and grow together as a team, raising your levels of fulfilment and overall happiness.

Here are our 10 key principles to use as a quick reminder during your parenting journey:

1. Focus on planning and prevention - instead of always being reactive.
2. Give empathy as often as possible - and do not discount feelings.
3. Model any behaviour you want to instil in your children - starting with respect and joy.
4. Use encouragement and descriptive praise - instead of general or evaluative praise.
5. Focus on what you can control - and don't undermine your authority with empty threats.

6. Allow your children to have some control over their lives - offer them limited choices and ask them questions.
7. Allow mistakes to happen - they are opportunities for learning.
8. Coach your children to own and solve their problems - and they will become self-responsible.
9. If you have to deliver consequences, do it with respect and empathy - and delay them when needed.
10. When you say or do something you regret, 'Rewind and Replay' and 'Repair' - to keep a strong connection with you children.

Final words and 'disclaimer':

Every child - and indeed family - is unique, with their own set of responses. If you find that you appear to be having limited success with a particular tool, do not despair! Children will often react negatively to changes in our parenting at first, but provided we are **consistent** and **patient** in our application of these new techniques, we almost always find that persistence pays off.

Please also bear in mind that some children pose challenges that require the help and knowledge of counsellors, doctors or psychiatrists and we do not claim to replace their expertise. So if you feel you might need this, please consult and get the help you need.

And above all, keep in mind that change needs repetition and practice! The fact is that all parents - including ourselves - can easily 'fall back' into old habits. It is therefore important to keep practicing and reminding yourself that even a small change to the way you react or speak to your children can make a huge difference over time.

Be your own best coach and remember that there is no such thing as a perfect parent - the fact that you read this book shows that you are willing to put time and effort into changing and making the difference in your family life.

Finally, to help you deal with the most typical challenging situations that might make you fall back into your old habits, we have selected the top 20 trouble-shooting scenarios in the next section. This gives you a quick reference guide with specific examples of how to use the tools in different situations. We recommend that you consult this any time a new challenge or behavioural change occurs - as they are bound to!

We're always here to help you make your parenting journey easier and more fulfilling, and we'd love to hear your stories - whether they are of struggles, success or failure, so please do share these by going to our website www.bestofparenting.com.

Coming up in

Appendix:

1. Refusing to cooperate
2. Refusing or making a fuss over homework
3. Siblings fighting about toys and physical possessions
4. Siblings using violence and teasing
5. Arguing
6. Whining
7. Tantrums
8. Shopping struggles
9. Hassling-Pestering Behaviour
10. Ignoring me
11. Not wanting to go to bed or to sleep
12. Negative attitude
13. Being 'bossy'
14. 'Back-talking', being rude and swearing
15. Lying or Fabricating
16. Wanting constant attention
17. Disrespecting house rules
18. Feeling insecure or lacking confidence
19. Taking too long to do everything
20. Hooked on Screens, TV, iPads and other game tablets

Appendix - Trouble-shooting top 20 parenting challenges

Refusing to cooperate

The voice of a child

I used to feel that all I heard from my parents was "Do this! Do that!", "No, not like that", which often made me feel like I couldn't do anything right. My parents bossed me about the whole time and it made me feel I didn't matter, and that whatever I had to say was not important, because Mum and Dad always knew better. So sometimes, just to get my voice heard and get my parent's attention I will refuse to do as I'm told, or shout "NO!", or do something I know that I shouldn't be doing.

Refusing to do what I am told is like saying to them "I am here! So why don't you give me some of your time and attention to enjoy each other, rather than always spending time on grown up things?" And although I hate being called 'naughty', it feels like fun to be able to control Dad's tone of voice and the colour of Mum's face!

The voice of the All-heart parent

I used to find it really hard to know how to deal with my kids when they were being defiant. I wanted to guide them towards better behaviour without pleading or cajoling, but found it easier said than done! It was reassuring to realise that it is normal for all our kids to go through phases of defiance or 'back talk'. Children are often inclined to 'test the boundaries' in order that they can learn about the world around them (and to see how much control they can have over it!). But I also knew that it was my role to show my children where these boundaries lay; otherwise, they'd grow up thinking that 'anything goes'. It was how to do it that I really needed help with and that, which I found in these tools.

The voice of the Strict parent

I expect my children to always listen, respect and obey me. So when they started to defy me, I began referring to them as 'naughty' children who needed to be disciplined. However, having researched child psychology, including age appropriate behaviour, I learnt that labelling children, with either 'good' or 'bad' labels is unhelpful and can lead to children believing in this definition, and hence reinforcing their behaviour. I also realised that my authoritarian response to their behaviour could 'backfire' on me when my children reached adolescence, the age at which children usually become rebellious and resentful of very strict parents. I am now more flexible towards my children, because I learnt that I do not have to solve every situation 'on the spot'.

Quick and easy solutions: ⏳ 5 minutes max

1. Limited Choices

- This is our favourite and most effective tool to encourage cooperation. It works for most situations and ages.
- Rather than making immediate 'demands' on your children, ask them to choose between two options (that suit *you*).
- Example: "Do you want to do this now or in a couple of minutes?"
- This has the advantage of putting our children into 'thinking mode' rather than 'opposition mode'.
- You should use 'Limited Choices' as often as you can, because asking children to participate in the decision-making allows them to feel some control over their lives and reduces conflict.

2. 'I' Statements

- If you focus on what you *can* control versus what you would *like* to control, you can then make a statement that you can actually enforce.
- Your 'I' Statement needs to start with an 'I' or 'My' (and if speaking for the family or couple, it starts with 'We' or 'Our').

- This tool replaces nagging and threatening with respectful communication. It also works with spouses!
- For example: say to your child gently, "I take children to the park *(or to wherever they want to go)* who have done ... *(whatever you want them to do)*".
- Notice that this sentence is positive and not a typical: "If you don't do this, you won't be able to do that!" threat.
- Keep in mind that your 'I' Statement must not be seen as an 'empty threat'. Your child needs to know that you mean what you say and that there will be consequences if they choose not to comply.

3. Setting Rules

- Set it in the third person and 'frame' it positively as this makes it less confrontational and increases the chances of your child respecting the rule.
- For e.g. 'Children who want to eat desert need to finish their lunch", rather than 'Children who don't finish their lunch won't get ice cream."
- Other e.g.: "This is the new rule: in this house, children have to tidy their room by the end of each day."
- If your child doesn't follow the rule, you can then impose a related consequence (see below).

Solutions requiring a little more time or practice:

While we have outlined examples for each tool below, it is best to refer to the full step-by-step explanation of each tool. To do so, please click on the tool title or go to the book index to find the corresponding tool.

1. Logical Consequences

Remember, this is not a punishment, when your child knows that a rule or agreement exists and then chooses to break it, you can apply a Related and Reasonable consequence with empathy. For example: "Sadly, since you haven't tidied your room you are going to have to stay and tidy it now rather than going to the park."

2. Delayed Consequences (4+)

When you can't apply a 'Logical Consequence' due to circumstance, or because you feel too angry or upset, you can delay it until a later time or date. Remember, this is not a punishment, so the consequence should be reasonable (and ideally related) and delivered with empathy. For example say at a later date: "You remember how I said I would keep the toys I picked up if you didn't tidy your room? Well, it's such a shame, but I had to pick them up."

3. Energy Drain (3+)

Example: "Seeing this untidy room at the end of the day gives me an energy drain".

4. Problem Solving (3+)

At a later time when your child is on his or her own with you, you can say something along the lines of: "When you refuse to do things that we agreed together, it doesn't give me much incentive to do things for you. What could we do to make sure this doesn't happen again?" And then begin a 'Problem Solving' session with your child.

Refusing or making a fuss over homework

The voice of a child

When I first started to get homework, I felt like I couldn't really do it on my own, so my Mum helped me. And now that the homework is getting more difficult and making me quite anxious, I nag my Mum until she agrees to help me. But when she's away, I'm in trouble because my Dad says that I need to do my homework on my own and stop depending on my Mum. He isn't at all sympathetic and doesn't seem to understand that I can become anxious when I don't know how to do something. He tells me he isn't ever going to help me, not one teensy bit and that unless I do my homework, I won't be able to do lots of fun things. So now I'm just confused and worried about what I'm going to do? I really hate my homework. I think I might give up on it just to show them!

The voice of the All-heart parent

I used to be tempted to help my kids with their homework in order to take the stress out of the situation both for them and for me. But I realised that my intervention merely made things worse in the long run because they were becoming dependent on my help. Smaller children certainly need support to learn to do their homework on their own, so we should offer them our help. And sometimes we have to reassure a child who has become overly anxious about their homework. However, it is really important to make children responsible for their homework as early as possible, so that it doesn't become a constant battle and source of stress.

The voice of the Strict parent

I used to get frustrated by the drama that seemed to come with the arrival of homework in my kids' lives. Without my realising it, this frustration usually caused a 'vicious' circle as my irritation made them even less able to do their homework, causing me to become even more frustrated. Yet even after I started realising the negative effect my reaction was having, I still found it hard to change my behaviour, which was really sad! It is only when I started applying some of the tools below that I was able to make my child less anxious, and more capable of doing their homework on their own.

Quick and easy solutions: ⏳ 5 minutes max
1. Empathy and Validation

- Giving children some empathy should always be the first step before helping them redirect their emotions. When a child feels understood they are encouraged to want to listen to what we have to say.
- For example: "You seem to be upset about your homework."

2. Limited Choices

- For example: "Would you like to do your homework now or after having a snack?" or "Would you like to do your homework sitting beside me while I read or up in your own room?"
- When we give our children an opportunity to choose between two things (both of which suit us) we encourage them to make decisions for themselves.
- Not only will the act of making a choice distract them from their emotions, but it will also allow them to feel more empowered and responsible.
- It's also worth remembering that when children are given choices they move from 'opposition mode' into 'thinking mode', and become interested in listening rather than arguing.

3. 'I' Statements

- An 'I' statement is a non-negotiable and enforceable statement that we are in a position to enforce and it needs to start with 'I' or 'my' (and if speaking for the family or couple, it starts with 'we' or 'our').
- For example: say to your child gently, "I will take children who have finished their homework to their friend's house". Or if your child is asking for help with his/her homework: "I give ideas to children who have already started their homework."
- 'I' statements work because they provide clear, non-negotiable guidance.
- Keep in mind that your 'I' Statement must not be seen as an 'empty threat'. Your child needs to know that you mean what you say and that there will be consequences if they refuse to comply.

4. Setting Rules

- Setting rules helps, particularly when these rules apply to the whole family.
- For example "In this family we do our work before we play."

- When you set a rule make sure that you do it in the spirit of empathy so that it sounds like a guiding principal, rather than a reprimand.
- It also helps to explain to our children just why we are setting a particular rule, which includes putting it in context.

Solutions requiring a little more time or practice:

While we have outlined examples for each tool below, it is best to refer to the full step-by-step explanation of each tool. To do so, please click on the tool title or go to the book index to find the corresponding tool.

1. Logical Consequences

Remember, this is not a punishment. When your child knows that a rule or agreement exists and then chooses to break it, you can apply a Related and Reasonable consequence with empathy: "Sadly, you haven't done your homework yet, which means that you won't be able to watch TV."

2. Delayed Consequences (age 4+)

When you can't apply a 'Logical Consequence' due to circumstance, or because you feel too angry or upset, you can delay it until a later time or date. Remember, this is not a punishment, so the consequence should be reasonable (and ideally related) and delivered with empathy. For example say at a later date: "Sadly, last night you chose not to respect the 'do your homework' rule - that you had previously committed to - so we won't be able to go to the cinema tonight."

3. Energy Drain (age 3+)

Example: "All this hassle around homework is giving me an energy drain. How are you going to give me back some energy?"

4. Active Listening

Example: "There seems to be something that's worrying you about your homework this week. Would you like to have a chat about it before you start working?"

5. Generating Solutions (age 4+)

Example (to be used if your child is not too distressed to be able to hear you): "You seem to be struggling to settle down to do the homework you have been given, do you have any thoughts as to how you might be able to make it easier to start work?"

Siblings fighting about toys and physical possessions

The voice of a child

My brother can be the most annoying person in the world, particularly when he uses my toys without my permission. And it's really fun to get a reaction out of him by teasing him. But most of the time we get on ok. Sometimes we lose our temper with each other and although it can look like our fights get pretty serious, we usually manage to sort it out ourselves. But the problem is that when our parents see us fighting they either freak out or take sides. Nine times out of ten they take my little brother's side, which is really unfair! Of course he knows that they will almost always stand up for him, and has started picking fights with me just so that I can get blamed and punished! That makes me feel completely unloved and bullied by everyone. And when that happens I get angry with everyone and they get even angrier with me, and so on and on.

The voice of the All-heart Parent

How I used to 'hover' over my children when they were arguing! I was always trying to restore the peace between them by determining who got to play with what. What a waste of my time it was! But the fact is that siblings squabble; and in fact, arguing is a necessary learning experience for it allows them to learn how to resolve conflicts, and to appreciate important values such as sharing for themselves. However, I had to learn that children under the age of four usually find it difficult to share and that trying to force any child to share, regardless of their age, was counterproductive. I turned instead to teaching them the need for empathy, both by modelling it for them and by explaining its importance.

The voice of the Strict Parent

I used to try and referee my children's battles over their possessions, intervening, adjudicating and breaking up fights with harsh words and threats of punishment. That didn't solve anything as the fighting and reprimands only got worse! I learnt to intervene far less, which helped me see that most conflicts ended up resolving themselves without my intervention. I also learnt to focus on pre-empting these issues from happening by involving my children in the creation of our rules. Consulting with them in this way made it much more likely that they would want to follow 'their' rules in the future!

Quick and easy solutions: ⌛ 5 minutes max

1. Empathy and Validation

- Try not to intervene when your children are fighting (as long as they are not hitting each other seriously!).
- If they come to you whining about the fact that a brother or sister has done something wrong (as they will often do) give them empathy, but explain to them that they need to resolve things without your help.
- For example, simply tell them: "You seem to be bothered by what your brother did? I trust you to be able to resolve this with him."
- But keep an eye (or rather an ear, as you might decide to leave the room) on the fights, to ensure that none of the siblings is subjecting the other to unnecessary force or stress.

2. Setting Rules

- For example set 'Property rights' - house rules to clarify exactly what possession can be shared, when and who with.
- The trick is to set these limits in a non-confrontational way using the third person.

- If possible, encourage your children to participate in setting these limits so that they feel invested in the application of the rules. A family meeting is the perfect environment for instigating your children's involvement.
- You could also encourage your children to designate 'sacred' spaces or shelves, where each sibling has their own toys/possessions that the others may not touch. This sacred space could be a child's own room (if he or she is lucky enough to have a room of his or her own), or even a temporary area such as a carpet or a mat on the floor. The rule can be that when your child's toys lie outside of this 'sacred space', any sibling is permitted to use them and furthermore, that the 'owner' has to wait for the other to finish playing._
- If the rules are not followed, you will have to apply a consequence.

Solutions requiring a little more time or practice:

While we have outlined examples for each tool below, it is best to refer to the full step-by-step explanation of each tool. To do so, please click on the tool title or go to the book index to find the corresponding tool.

1. Logical Consequences

Remember, this is not a punishment. When your child knows that a rule or agreement exists and then chooses to break it, you can apply a Related and Reasonable consequence with empathy. For example: "This is so sad, I see that you don't seem to be able to play with this toy without fighting, so unfortunately I'm going to have to take it away for a while."

2. Delayed Consequences (age 4+)

When you can't apply a Logical Consequence due to circumstance, or because you feel too angry or upset, you can delay it until a later time or date. Remember, this is not a punishment because the consequence should be reasonable (and ideally related) and delivered with empathy. For example: "Sadly, after all that fighting between you and your sister this morning over this game meant that I had to take it away."

3. Energy Drain (age 3+)

Example: "All this fighting is giving me an energy drain."

4. Problem Solving (age 3+)

At a later, quieter time, you can say something along the lines of: "You seem to be fighting over possessions a lot, what do you think would make you most willing to share your toys with each other?" And then begin a 'Problem Solving' session with your children.

5. Family Meetings (age 4+)

Bring the sharing issue at hand to a family meeting and problem solve together as to how your children could resolve their fights over possessions (and avoid squabbling in the first place!).

Siblings using violence and teasing

The voice of a Child

My sister and I fight ...a lot. We also tease each other...a lot. But it doesn't mean that we are going to kill each other, it's just what us kids do! I mean we also play together in a really friendly way too. But do our parents understand this? They certainly don't seem to as every time my sister and I start arguing, or occasionally hit each other, they go crazy. My Mum wants to protect whoever she thinks is the one getting most hurt. And my Dad just wants to send us both to our rooms or threatens us with smacks, which is pretty strange since he's telling us not to hit each other.

The voice of the All-heart parent

I just couldn't bear it when I saw my beloved children laying in to one another like savage beasts. So I'd rush to intervene, trying to identify the 'aggressor' and comfort the 'victim'. Unfortunately, it is very difficult to know who really started a fight, and playing the 'referee' deprives children of the opportunity to learn the art of conflict resolution for themselves. I had to learn that however distressing it is to witness our children fighting with each other, it is totally normal, and to some extent necessary, for them to do so. Of course, that doesn't mean turning one's back on the battle and allowing them to hurt each other seriously!

The voice of the Strict parent

I find it really difficult not to intervene when my children fight (as is also the case with most other parents who come to our parenting courses), particularly when I feel that one sibling is being unfair to the other. In fact, I used to find myself wading into fights and pulling my children apart from each other. And then I realised I was actually using force to try to stop them using force. Hardly the way to get a pacifist's message across! Since then I have played a far more effective role as an interested, but rarely active, observer. My children are now much more likely to listen and learn from me when I give them suggestions as to how they could resolve some of their conflicts.

Quick and easy solutions: ⏳ 5 minutes max
1. Empathy and Validation
- Try not to intervene when your children are fighting (as long as they are not hitting each other seriously!).
- If they come to you whining about the fact that a brother or sister has done something wrong (as they will often do) tell them with empathy: "This fight seems to be upsetting you and I trust you to be able to resolve this on your own."
- Try not to identify an 'aggressor' - it rarely helps to take sides unless there is obvious bullying going on.
- But keep an eye (or rather an ear, as you might decide to leave the room!) on the fights, to ensure that none of the siblings is subjecting the other to unnecessary force or stress.

2. Setting Rules
- A rule needs to be set respectfully, it needs to be set in the third person and it has to be set in a non-threatening manner.

- The rule also needs to be explained.
- An example might be: "The new rule is: fighting/teasing is unacceptable in this house."
- The rule about using rules is that only one rule should be used at a time – and try not to invent them in the heat of the moment otherwise they will begin to sound like reprimands.
- Setting Rules works because the rules set a framework or a gold standard for all family members, rather than acting like reprimands.
- If your children 'break' the rule, you need to apply a logical or delayed consequence (see below) in order to keep the rule effective.

Solutions requiring a little more time or practice:

While we have outlined examples for each tool below, it is best to refer to the full step-by-step explanation of each tool. To do so, please click on the tool title or go to the book index to find the corresponding tool.

1. One-on-one Time
A good way to reduce any type of sibling rivalry is to give each of your children some special time one to one.

2. "Uh-oh" and Time-Away (age 2+)
When your child knows that a rule or agreement exists and then chooses to break it, say "Uh-oh" and, then say with empathy and without anger: "It seems like you may need some Time-Away", and then follow the step-by-step (and don't forget to give them choices!). If they have already had experience of Time-Away then you may find that saying "Uh-oh" is enough to redirect their behaviour.

3. Logical Consequences
Remember, this is not a punishment. When your child knows that a rule or agreement exists and then chooses to break it, you can apply a Related

and Reasonable consequence with empathy. For example: "It's a shame but children who fight and kick cannot accompany me to the store."

4. Delayed Consequences (age 4+)

When you can't apply a 'Logical Consequence' due to circumstance, or because you feel too angry or upset, you can delay it until a later time or date. Remember, this is not a punishment, so the consequence should be reasonable (and ideally related) and delivered with empathy. For example say at a later date: "It's quite sad, but given how you were fighting earlier, I now don't feel like taking you to your friends' house."

5. Energy Drain (age 3+)

Example: "Your fighting is giving me an energy drain, I will need your help restoring it."

6. Problem Solving (age 3+)

Sometime after the event, address who you have seen (as opposed to believe) to be the 'aggressor' by saying: "I can see that you felt angry enough to hit out, but you need to know that violence is not ok, it upsets everyone and doesn't solve anything. What can we do so that it doesn't happen again?" And then begin a 'Problem Solving' session with your child.

7. Family Meetings (age 4+)

The above problem solving session is best done in the context of a family meeting, where every family member can give their own ideas as to how the violence and teasing can be prevented in the future.

Arguing

The voice of a child

I find that arguing works because if I argue enough with my Mum, she usually gives in and lets me do what I want to do. However, when I start arguing with my Dad, he gets pretty mad at me. I find this unfair because I've seen him argue with other people including my brother and my Mum! Why is it that he's allowed to do something, but when I copy what he does, he tells me that I'm being really rude and horrible? As I am scared of his reaction, I try not to do argue with him. But if I do and he reacts badly, I run to my Mum and she usually protects me and tells my Dad to leave me alone.

The voice of the All-heart parent

It is very common for children of all ages (and adults too!) to become argumentative when they don't feel they have enough control over their lives. A 'soft' parent, like me, might be tempted to negotiate or 'give in', but this is actually a recipe for endless arguments! I have learned at my own expense that it's far more effective to work on preventing these arguments from occurring in the first place.

The voice of the Strict parent

It can be a shock to authoritarian parents like me to hear their children trying to argue their way into getting what they want. Luckily, there are highly effective, non-punitive ways to prevent getting sucked into this 'battle of wills', and of resolving an argument when it does occur. I also learnt that parents should guard against labelling their child 'argumentative' because it may lead them into 'owning' this identity and arguing with you even more!

Quick and easy solutions: ⌛ 5 minutes max
1. Limited Choices
- This is our favourite and most effective tool to encourage cooperation. It works for most situations and ages.
- Rather than making immediate 'demands' on our children, ask them to choose between two options (that suit *you*).
- Example: "Do you want to leave the park now or in five minutes?"
- This has the advantage of putting your children into 'thinking mode' rather than 'opposition mode'.

- You should use 'Limited Choices' as often as you can, because asking children to make decisions allows them to feel some control over their lives, and therefore makes them less prone to being argumentative.

2. Positive Redirection
- To prevent arguments and power struggles, it's important to try and always answer your children's requests positively (although this doesn't mean agreeing!), and then redirect their request and/or offer an alternative.
- For example, instead of saying "No you can't go to the park, and you know perfectly why: you still haven't done your homework!", you can say instead "Sure we can go to the park once you have finished your homework", or alternatively "Sure we can go to the park tomorrow as you need to finish your homework today."

Solutions requiring a little more time or practice:
While we have outlined examples for each tool below, it is best to refer to the full step-by-step explanation of each tool. To do so, please click on the tool title or go to the book index to find the corresponding tool.

1. Diffusing Whining and Arguing (age 3+)
Example: say to your child as soon as s/he starts arguing about something: "I know", or "I heard you", or "I love you too much to argue", and simply repeat this statement with empathy and without getting angry until they realise that you're not going to give in.

2. Logical Consequences
Remember, this is not a punishment. When your child knows that a rule or agreement exists and then chooses to break it, you can apply a Related and Reasonable consequence with empathy: "As you know, in this house, those who argue get less than what they were asking for in the first place, so we have to leave your friends' house even earlier."

3. Delayed Consequences (age 4+)

When you can't apply a Logical Consequence due to circumstance, or because you feel too angry or upset, you can delay it until a later time or date. Remember, this is not a punishment because the consequence should be reasonable (and ideally related) and delivered with empathy. For example: "Sadly, when you started arguing with me in the shop last time we were buying you clothes it put me off wanting to go shopping with you, so I will go shopping alone today, but there is always another time."

4. Energy Drain (age 3+)

Example: "All this arguing really gives me an energy drain, how are you going to put energy back into Mummy?"

5. Problem Solving

At a later time when your child is on his or her own with you, you can say something along the lines of: "Don't you think arguing like this prevents us both from doing lots of more enjoyable things together? What could we do to reduce the amount of time we spend arguing?" And then begin a 'Problem Solving' session with your child.

Whining

The voice of a child

I often use whining to get something I want because it just seems the best way to get it! If I pull hard enough on my Mum or Dad's sleeve and use my wheedling voice for long enough they usually give in, especially when they are busy with something else. And if I want to go to the park or get a new toy, I make sure that I've made enough noise with my voice so that they agree to take me, just to get me to be quiet. Sure one of them might get cross, but usually I get my way in the end.

The voice of The All-heart Parent

If you have a child who never whines, you can really consider yourself lucky, as I haven't met one yet! But knowing that whining is totally normal doesn't mean we should just 'give in' to it for the sake of stopping it as I once did. The fact is that children will continue doing what 'works' for them. It's up to us to show them that there are better and more effective ways of asking for what they want.

The voice of the Strict parent

My own exasperation is 'triggered' by the sound of a whining child. This usually leads us into a vicious cycle as my reactions only worsen the situation. My big 'Aha moment' was when I realised that, rather than screaming "Stop whining!" at my children, I could just avoid getting 'emotionally engaged' in their whining in the first place.

Quick and easy solutions: ⏳ 5 minutes max

1. 'I' Statements

- If we focus on what we can control versus what we would like to control, we can then make a statement that we can actually enforce.
- Our 'I' Statement needs to start with an 'I' or 'My' (and if speaking for the family or couple, it starts with 'We' or 'Our').
- This tool replaces nagging and threatening with respectful communication. It also works with spouses!
- For example, gently tell your child "I listen to children who speak in the same tone of voice as mine."
- Notice that this sentence is positive and not a typical: "If you don't do that, you won't be able to do that!" threat.
- Keep in mind that your 'I' Statement must not be seen as an 'empty threat'. Your child needs to know that you mean what you say and that there will be consequences if they refuse to comply.

2. Positive Redirection

- To prevent arguments and power struggles, it's important to always try to answer your children's requests positively (although this doesn't mean agreeing!), and then redirect their request or offer an alternative.
- For example: "I won't be giving you a chocolate bar at this time of day, but I can give you an apple."

3. Setting Rules

- Set it in the third person as this makes it less confrontational and increases the chances of your child respecting the rule.
- Example: "This is the new rule: in this house, children who whine don't get what they are asking for."
- If your child doesn't follow the rule, you can then impose a related consequence (see below).

Solutions requiring a little more time or practice:

While we have outlined examples for each tool below, it is best to refer to the full step-by-step explanation of each tool. To do so, please click on the tool title or go to the book index to find the corresponding tool.

1. Diffusing Whining and Arguing (age 3+)

Respond to your child by repeating an 'empathetic statement' like "I know", or "I heard you", or "I love you too much to argue". Say this as often as needed and without giving in, getting angry or raising your voice.

2. Logical Consequences

Remember, this is not a punishment. When your child knows that a rule or agreement exists and then chooses to break it, you can apply a Related and Reasonable consequence with empathy. For example: "I know that you want an ice cream, but sadly the rule in this house is that children who whine cannot get what they are asking for."

3. Delayed Consequences (age 4+)

When you can't apply a Logical Consequence due to circumstance, or because you feel too angry or upset, you can delay it until a later time or date. Remember, this is not a punishment because the consequence should be reasonable (and ideally related) and delivered with empathy. For example: "Sadly, since you carried on whining at me in the car I now don't feel like watching our TV programme together."

4. Energy Drain (age 3+)

Example: "All this whining is causing me an energy drain, I'll need your help getting some energy back."

5. Problem Solving (age 3+)

At a later time when your child is on his or her own with you, you can say something along the lines of: "When you ask for something the way you did this morning, do you think it makes me want to give it to you? Whining doesn't work in this house, so what would be a better way of asking?" and follow through with a Problem Solving session.

Tantrums

The voice of a child

I know that I have tantrums and do you know what? I feel that sometimes it's the only way to get noticed. But sometimes, when I'm having a tantrum I don't even know what's happening to me and it feels quite scary. When I have a tantrum, my Mum starts giving me lots of attention and sweets or other things to make me feel better. So it kinda makes me want to have more tantrums to get more attention and more treats. However, my Dad seems to believe that I am doing it all on purpose to annoy him and gets very angry, which just makes me feel even more upset.

The voice of the All-heart parent

It really helps to know that regular tantrums are normal in young children from the age of 18 months to four years. When my eldest daughter had her first 'full-blown' temper tantrum, I felt horrified. What was happening to her? I'd hover over her trying to help, but it only made things worse. My third child started having tantrums from as early as 15 months old. Thankfully, I have now learnt to stop being so affected by her strong emotions and can focus on calmly getting her back on track.

The voice of the Strict parent

I really didn't know how to deal with tantrums as I thought that if I didn't stop them, my child would think that this type of behaviour was acceptable. Once I understood that temper tantrums are just a young brain expressing frustration at not being able to process strong emotions, I was much better equipped to help my children out of their distress, rather than adding to it. It is what we do before and after tantrums occur, rather than while they are actually happening, that helps reduce their frequency. However, I also made clear to my children that outbursts were not an acceptable way to get what they want.

Quick and easy solutions: ⌛ 5 minutes max
1. Planning Ahead
- Primary causes of tantrums are tiredness, hunger, lack of activity, or sudden changes in environment.
- It is easy to forget just how much sleep children of all ages need, particularly when they don't like to admit to tiredness or are unable to recognise their own fatigue. The signs of fatigue can be confusing because tired children may present as 'hyper' rather than sleepy.
- So when anticipating possible tantrums, make sure that you have addressed your kids' basic needs first.

2. Limited Choices
- This is our favourite and most effective tool to encourage cooperation. It works for most situations and ages.

- Rather than making immediate 'demands' on our children, we ask them to choose between two options (that suit us).
- Example: "I am hearing that you really want to eat ice cream, would you like to eat it after dinner or tomorrow after lunch?" Or "I can see you really want this toy, would you like to put it on your Birthday wish list or on your list for Santa?"
- This has the advantage of putting our children into 'thinking mode' and it makes it easier for them to get out of their tantrum.
- We should use 'Limited Choices' as often as we can, because asking children to make decisions allows them to feel some control over their lives, and therefore makes them less prone to power struggles.

3. Empathy and Validation

- Even if we think that our children can't hear us over the sound of their own wails, it's worth trying to get close to them just to let them know that we care.
- Say to your child with empathy "I can see you are very upset..."
- However unnerving tantrums may be, we should try to provide a quiet, peaceful response (and atmosphere if possible) when they do occur.
- At the same time, hold steadfast to your own rules and try hard not to 'give in'. In this way our children will learn that tantrums are not the way to get what they want.

4. Big Hug

- Hugging almost always helps reassure and calm down distressed children.
- You can even call hugging 'The Big Hug Time' and refer to it whenever your child loses control.
- For example. Tell your child "I'm going to hug you until you calm down because I love you, and I don't want you to hurt yourself or anyone else."

- If your child is really frustrated or upset, he or she may lose physical control, which may involve striking out at you or others. If you can get near your child without getting hurt, or without too much of a struggle, keep trying to hold them in your arms until the tantrum stops.
- If your child is in a public place (for example in the middle of a supermarket), you should lead him or her to a quiet place, such as the car or a rest room and keep him or her safe until the tantrum has ended.

5. Positive Redirection

- To prevent power struggles and tantrums, it's important to try and always answer your children's requests positively (although this doesn't mean agreeing!), and then redirect their request and/or offer an alternative.
- For example, instead of saying "No! You can't have an ice cream as you haven't had lunch yet", say: "Sure, you can have this ice cream after lunch."

Solutions requiring a little more time or practice:

While we have outlined examples for each tool below, it is best to refer to the full step-by-step explanation of each tool. To do so, please click on the tool title or go to the book index to find the corresponding tool.

1. Diffusing Whining and Arguing (age 3+)

Example: tell your child: "I can see that you really, really want that toy, but unfortunately, it's not going to be possible" and follow any whining or arguing with an empathetic statement such as: "I heard you", or "I know", or …

2. Problem Solving (age 3+)

At a later time when your child is on his or her own with you, you can say something along the lines of: "When you throw yourself on the floor because you want something, it doesn't make me want to give it to you, what do you think would be a better way to ask me for something?" And then begin a 'Problem Solving' session with your child.

Shopping struggles

If your child is younger than three, see also the solutions to "Tantrums"

The voice of a child

I know that I am supposed to behave well when we are out and about, but sometimes it's difficult. Shops are so full of things that I really, really want, especially things that I see in adverts or at my friend's houses, things that look so cool! I wish my parents would understand that I'm trying to behave how they'd like me to, but sometimes I forget, especially when I feel like I really want something. And I'm never sure how to behave because one day my Mum will give in to my requests (if I nag her enough!) and on another she won't, so I always end up trying to wheedle something out of her just in case she is having one of her 'generous days'.

The voice of the All-heart parent

Most shops are designed to make us all want to buy things and children are easy targets. For the sake of a smooth exit or an easy life I confess I often gave in to my children's demands for stuff! However, this was always a subject of disagreement with my husband because he felt I wasn't teaching our kids the 'real value' of things, and that they would become 'spoilt', or feel 'entitled'. Learning that one can stand one's ground without resorting to a power struggle brings great benefits, not least a reduction in the amount one gets pestered.

The voice of the Strict parent

What I realised as a parent who had little tolerance towards being constantly asked by my children to buy them things, was that my children were far more likely to stop hassling me if I met their demands with a bit of empathy rather than a reprimand. This doesn't mean that one has to agree, far from it, it just means that acknowledging your child's feelings, and then redirecting their demand, is far more effective than a stern "NO!".

Quick and easy solutions: ⌛ 5 minutes max

1. Planning Ahead

- Before the shopping trip, agree with your child what the rules are.
- Example: if you're willing to buy them something: "I am willing to buy you one sweet, toy or magazine that costs less than £3."
- Example: if you're not willing to buy them anything: "I am happy to take you to the supermarket, so long as you do not ask me to buy you anything while we're there".
- Optionally: you can also let them know what will happen if they start whining/hassling. For example: "If you start asking me for things, we'll have to leave the supermarket." But if you do, you have to make sure that you follow through if it happens!

2. 'I' Statements

- Focus on what you can control without issuing a threat.
- Example: before going to the supermarket: "I will take children shopping who don't constantly ask me to buy things."
- Example: while at the supermarket: "I buy things to children who ask me without whining and who are capable of respecting me when I say "No".

3. Positive Redirection

- To prevent arguments and power struggles, it's important to try to always answer your children's requests positively (although this doesn't mean agreeing!), and then redirect their request and/ or offer an alternative.

- Example: "Sure you can buy it, as long as you can pay it with your allowance" (for children who receive allowances), or "Would you rather add it to your birthday or Christmas wish list?"

4. Pocket Money/Allowance

- Try and give them a sense of the value of money and the importance of saving early on (typically from the age of five), by giving them a small weekly allowance.
- You can then refer to this allowance any time they want something new by saying to them: "I'm happy for you to buy this, as long as you pay for it with your own pocket money."

5. Setting Rules

- Set it in the third person.
- Example: "This is the rule: children who want to come to the supermarket cannot whine or argue to ask for things."
- If your child doesn't follow the rule, you can then impose a logical consequence (see below).

Solutions requiring a little more time or practice:

While we have outlined examples for each tool below, it is best to refer to the full step-by-step explanation of each tool. To do so, please click on the tool title or go to the book index to find the corresponding tool.

1. Logical Consequences

Remember, this is not a punishment. When your child knows that a rule or agreement exists and then chooses to break it, you can apply a Related and Reasonable consequence with empathy. For example: "It's really sad, but since you are not following our agreement, we will have to put back the nice stuff we found and leave the shop."

2. Delayed Consequences (4+)

When you can't apply a 'Logical Consequence' due to circumstance, or because you feel too angry or upset, you can delay it until a later time or date. Remember, this is not a punishment, so the consequence should be reasonable (and ideally related) and delivered with empathy. For example, say at a later date: "I'd love to take you to the supermarket, but unfortunately, given how you behaved last time *(try to be more specific if you can)*, I'm not going to be able to, maybe next time."

3. Energy Drain (3+)
Example: "Your hassling me is draining me of energy." And you then ask your children how they are going to give you back some energy (for example doing house chores).

4. Problem Solving (3+)
At a later time when your child is on his or her own with you, you can say something along the lines of: "I'm sure you don't like it when your sister begs you repeatedly for something and then throws a scene. Well I don't like it when you do it either. What would be a better way of dealing with this when we're at the supermarket?" And you then do a 'Problem Solving' session with them.

Hassling-Pestering Behaviour

The voice of a child
If I really want something I will wait until the right moment to hassle my Mum and Dad for it. So for example, I will say 'I'm not going to move from here unless you agree to buy me the toy I want', and I keep on at them until they agree. It usually works with my Mum and she gives in. However, my Dad usually gets quite angry and starts screaming so I know that I might get a punishment rather than a reward, but it's still worth the risk isn't it?

The voice of The All-heart Parent
When my children used to pester me I would find it difficult not to give in to them, eventually – which just lead to more hassling in the future.

So I started asking myself why they were hassling me in the first place, and realised that it was usually because they would get away with it. Once I decided to become more consistent and set some limits, I had to find a better alternative to just switching to "No!".

The voice of The Strict Parent

Being able to recognise the way we react to our children often provides the key to controlling the way they behave towards us. I had to learn that if I was in the habit of using nagging to get my own way, my children were likely to copy my behaviour and nag or hassle me themselves! I had to learn to be less emotionally involved in order to be able to set limits effectively.

Quick and easy solutions: ⌛ 5 minutes max

1. Empathy and Validation

- Ask your child what they want from you, and listen carefully to their answer, then reflect back what you have heard, then offer reassurance.
- For example: "It sounds like you would like to spend some time with me, shall we have a bit of 'One-on-one Time' as soon as I finish what I am doing?"

2. Positive Redirection

- To prevent arguments and power struggles, it's important to always try to answer your children's requests positively (although this doesn't mean agreeing!), and then redirect their request or offer an alternative.
- For example: "Yes, you can have this chocolate bar, but you'll have to wait for snack time."

Solutions requiring a little more time or practice:

While we have outlined examples for each tool below, it is best to refer to the full step-by-step explanation of each tool. To do so, please click on the tool title or go to the book index to find the corresponding tool.

1. Diffusing Whining and Arguing (age 3+)

Example: "I can see that you really, really want me to take you to the soft play centre, but unfortunately, it's not going to be possible now." And then repeat an 'empathetic statement' like "I know", or "I heard you", or "I love you too much to argue".

2. Delayed Consequences (age 4+)

When you can't apply a Logical Consequence due to circumstance, or because you feel too angry or upset, you can delay it until a later time or date. Remember, this is not a punishment because the consequence should be reasonable (and ideally related) and delivered with empathy.

3. Energy Drain (age 3+)

Example: "All this arguing is causing me an energy drain, I'll need your help getting some energy back."

4. Problem Solving (3+)

At a later time when your child is on his or her own with you, you can say something along the lines of: "You have been constantly asking for things today and it has become pretty annoying. What do you think would be a better way of getting my attention?"And then begin a 'Problem Solving' session with your child.

Ignoring me

The voice of a child

When you are small like me, the world can seem a bit big, noisy and scary with too much going on that is really hard to understand. Sometimes it seems that adults spend the whole time shouting or pointing at me to *do* stuff or *be* a certain way. It hurts my feelings when they repeat themselves and treat me like I didn't hear them or like I'm stupid. So to show them that they aren't always the 'boss' of me, I just stop listening and ignore them.

The voice of the All-heart parent

As a protective parent I like to feel close to my kids, both physically and emotionally, so when they ignored me I used to feel frustrated and saddened. It came as a relief to know that it is normal for kids to have bursts of playing the 'I am ignoring you' game or just phases of showing their parents less attention. Once I learned how to reconnect with my kids, including getting them to listen to me, these periods of 'switching off' presented far less of a worry or threat.

The voice of the Strict parent

In the past I used to get very angry if my children ignored me, and I would tell them so in no uncertain terms. But then I realised that my authoritarian attitude was sometimes the very reason why they were ignoring me in the first place, as it can be discouraging to always be bossed around. The fact is that kids always learn better when we are 'modelling' the kind of behaviour we'd like them to adopt – it is much more effective than just ordering them to do something in a 'Because *I* say so!' manner.

Quick and easy solutions: ⧗ 5 minutes max
1. Respectful Communication

- Try speaking to a child by getting down to his or her level, rather than screaming an order from a distance (which we all do from time to time!), it often works a treat.
- If we want to be even more effective, we can try whispering, children love anything that resembles a secret.
- Also, if we use **Modelling** and **Humour,** even when our children are ignoring us, we teach them a better alternative to their behaviour.

2. 'I' Statements

- If we focus on what we *can* control versus what we would *like* to control, we can then make a statement that we can actually enforce.
- Our 'I' Statement needs to start with an 'I' or 'My' (and if speaking for the family or couple, it starts with 'We' or 'Our').
- This tool replaces nagging and threatening with respectful communication. It also works with spouses!
- For example: tell your child gently, "I listen to children who listen to me".
- Notice that this sentence is positive and not a typical: "If you don't do that, you won't be able to do that!" threat.
- Keep in mind that your 'I' Statement must not be seen as an 'empty threat'. Your child needs to know that you mean what you say and that there will be consequences if they refuse to comply.

3. Limited Choices

- This is our favourite and most effective tool to encourage cooperation. It works for most situations and ages.
- Rather than making immediate 'demands' on our children, we ask them to choose between two options (that suit us).
- For example: "Would you rather do this now, or after you've finished your drawing?"
- This has the advantage of putting our children into 'thinking mode' rather than 'opposition mode'.
- We should use 'Limited Choices' as often as we can, because asking children to make decisions allows them to feel some control over their lives, and therefore makes them less prone to power struggles.

4. Setting Rules

- Set it in the third person.
- For e.g. "This is the new rule: in this house, we do things for children who listen to us."

- If your child doesn't follow the rule, you can them impose a related consequence (see below).

Solutions requiring a little more time or practice:

While we have outlined examples for each tool below, it is best to refer to the full step-by-step explanation of each tool. To do so, please click on the tool title or go to the book index to find the corresponding tool.

1. Logical Consequences

Remember, this is not a punishment. When your child knows that a rule or agreement exists and then chooses to break it, you can apply a Related and Reasonable consequence with empathy. For example: "Sadly, because you have chosen not to listen to me, I'm not going to be able to play with you right now."

2. Delayed Consequences (age 4+)

When you can't apply a 'Logical Consequence' due to circumstance, or because you feel too angry or upset, you can delay it until a later time or date. Remember, this is not a punishment, so the consequence should be reasonable (and ideally related) and delivered with empathy. For example, say at a later date: "Sadly, because you chose not to listen to me earlier on we now won't be able to go and get an ice cream."

3. Energy Drain (age 3+)

Example: "I am not feeling listened to and that is draining my energy, and so I no longer have enough energy to take you to the park."

4. Problem Solving (age 3+)

At a later time when your child is on his or her own with you, you can say something along the lines of: "When you appear to ignore me, I feel disrespected and upset. What could we do to make sure this doesn't happen again?" And then begin a 'Problem Solving' session with your child.

Not wanting to go to bed or to sleep

The voice of a child

If someone shouts at you "Stop messing about and go to sleep NOW!", are you able to calm down and obey them immediately? Well, then you won't be surprised to learn that neither can I. My parents don't seem to understand that it just isn't as easy as they think to fall asleep on my own. I hate having to go to bed, especially when other people are allowed to stay up and do fun things. So sometimes I make a fuss so that I don't have to go to bed straightaway, and sometimes my 'staying up tricks' work and I'm allowed to stay downstairs and watch TV or eat a snack. Sometimes I cry out that I need a drink, or that I'm scared, or that there is a noisy fly in my room. Sometimes Mum and Dad come and try and settle me down and sing to me, so that makes me think that making a fuss is a good way of getting attention, so I do it again! But sometimes they get really angry with me and then shut me in my room or take away my privileges. The thing about my parents is that you never know how they will react.

The voice of the Strict parent

Do you believe, as I used to, that you can control when your kids sleep? In the old days I found the going to sleep process (or absence of it) very challenging indeed, and tended to encourage my children's wakeful state by getting annoyed with them. But once I looked into the whole sleep issue I saw that children avoid sleep for many reasons, ranging from having too much fun to night fears. The key to solving our children's sleep issues lies in understanding why it is that they won't go to sleep. For younger children, often a nightlight might be the key, or leaving the door open, or moving to that bigger bed, or moving back into their old room for a while. Once I stood back to work out my children's state of mind and address it accordingly, I found that they were much more willing to fall asleep unaided. Punishing them for refusing to abide by an overly strict sleep routine will only cause further problems.

The voice of the All-heart parent

During the early years of parenting, I spent hours upon hours trying to coax my child to sleep, and yet my efforts were often unsuccessful, so I'd accept that she would sleep in our bed. In the end, I got fed up with feeling exhausted and frustrated so I began to look at the research. I realised that my approach to the pre-bed wind-down routine was all-important. Once I had put in place a nightly routine, combined with clear boundaries delivered with empathy, all my children found it much easier to acclimatise themselves to the whole business of saying goodbye to the day and drifting off to sleep.

Quick and easy solutions: ⏳ 5 minutes max

1. Limited Choices

- This is our favourite and most effective tool to encourage cooperation. It works for most situations and ages.
- Rather than making immediate 'demands' on our children, we ask them to choose between two options (that suit *us*).
- Example: "Would you like to go to bed now or in ten minutes?" or "Would you like me to help you up to bed or would you like to go on your own?"
- This has the advantage of putting our children into 'thinking mode' rather than 'opposition mode'.
- We should use 'Limited Choices' as often as we can, because asking children to make decisions allows them to feel some control over their lives, and therefore makes them less prone to power struggles.

2. 'I' Statements

- If we focus on what we can control versus what we would like to control, we can then make a statement that we can actually enforce.
- Our 'I' Statement needs to start with an 'I' or 'My' (and if speaking for the family or couple, it starts with 'We' or 'Our').

- This tool replaces nagging and threatening with respectful communication. It also works with spouses!
- For example: say to your child gently, "I sing lullabies to children who go to bed." Notice that this sentence is positive and not a typical: "If you don't do that, you won't be able to do that!" threat.
- If your child still refuses to listen to you, repeat your statement and if they ask for something, appear to ignore their request for a little while.

3. Setting Rules

- Set it in the third person as this makes it less confrontational and increases the chances of your child respecting the rule.
- For example: "The new rule is: 'grown up's time begins at 8pm, which means that children need to remain in their room, even if they decide not to go to sleep immediately.'"
- As long as children don't come out of their room, it may be an option to let them go to sleep a bit later if they wish to. Or to wake at the usual time so that they feel the result of their decision, i.e. feeling tired the next day.
- However, we need to ensure that our children don't have access to screens, don't keep younger siblings awake, and understand that they mustn't leave their room.
- If your child doesn't follow the rule, you can then impose a related consequence (see below).

Solutions requiring a little more time or practice:

While we have outlined examples for each tool below, it is best to refer to the full step-by-step explanation of each tool. To do so, please click on the tool title or go to the book index to find the corresponding tool.

1. Creating Routines

Devise a 'going to sleep' ritual with your child (a prayer, poem or lullaby often helps calm a child).

2. Logical Consequences

Remember, this is not a punishment. When your child knows that a rule or agreement exists and then chooses to break it, you can apply a Related and Reasonable consequence with empathy: "Sadly, since you are choosing not to get into bed I am going to have to read you a shorter story tonight."

3. Delayed Consequences (age 4+)

When you can't apply a 'Logical Consequence' due to circumstance, or because you feel too angry or upset, you can delay it until a later time or date. Remember, this is not a punishment, so the consequence should be reasonable (and ideally related) and delivered with empathy. For example, say at a later date: "It's really sad, but since you wouldn't stay in bed the other night, you need to go to bed earlier tonight so I can't allow you to watch TV."

4. Energy Drain (age 3+)

Tell your child, for example: "All this dithering about is causing me an energy drain, I'll need your help getting some energy back."

5. Problem Solving (age 3+)

At a later time when your child is on his or her own with you, you can say something along the lines of: "It makes me frustrated when you won't get into bed at the right time because it means that the next day you are tired, less able to concentrate and moody. What do you think you could do about this?" And then begin a 'Problem Solving' session with your child.

Negative attitude

The voice of a child

Sometimes I feel like I just can't get anything right because all I seem to get from my parents is criticism or negatives, "No!...", "Stop doing that! ...", "You mustn't! …", "You can't! …", "Why didn't you…?" And then after hearing all that negativity from them they actually accuse me of being negative towards them?! I wish they'd understand that sometimes I'm happy and sometimes I'm a bit sad or cross. Yes I'm a bit grumpy sometimes, but that's allowed isn't it? Do I always have to be happy and good?

The voice of the All-heart parent

I felt really sad when my children appeared to be 'down' on anything; whether life, others or even themselves. I wanted to make sure that they were happy all the time, so I'd tell them to always look at the bright side of things and that things were not as bad as they seemed to think. I never realised that I was actually discounting their feelings by doing that, and that I needed to use more effective techniques.

The voice of the Strict parent

All children go through negative phases, particularly as they are approaching adolescence. I used to hate it when my daughters were being negative and would tell them so… until I noticed that I was meeting their negativity with more of the same! Above all never brand a child 'negative', not only is it a very negative thing to do in itself, but they may also start assuming that negativity is part of their identity and start acting accordingly!

NB: If a child is consistently 'down' on life despite applying some tried and tested tools, it may be worth investigating whether he or she is experiencing depression, a clinical condition rather than a voluntary behaviour.

Quick and easy solutions: ⌛ 5 minutes max

1. Acknowledgement and Encouragement

- If your child has a negative attitude, try to encourage and praise them on what they are doing well. Research shows that 80% of parents' interaction with their children is based around negative comments and criticism, both of which are often done so unconsciously.
- However, keep in mind that praise has to be descriptive. Instead of praising them with general words such as 'Good boy', try and

describe something specific that he or she has done, or show interest in your child's achievement by asking questions about what he or she accomplished in the particular task.

- Also, it is much better to praise the effort than praising the person. For e.g. "You've done well, you must have put a lot of effort into this" is much better than, "You've done well, you're really clever."

2. Limited Choices

- This is our favourite and most effective tool to encourage cooperation. It works for most situations and ages.
- Rather than making immediate 'demands' on our children, we ask them to choose between two options (that suit *us).*
- For example: "Which of these two fun things would you like to do …?"
- This has the advantage of putting our children into 'thinking mode' rather than 'opposition mode'.
- We should use 'Limited Choices' as often as we can, because asking children to make decisions allows them to feel some control over their lives, and therefore makes them less prone to power struggles.

3. 'I' Statements

- If we focus on what we can control versus what we would like to control, we can then make a statement that we can actually enforce.
- Our 'I' Statement needs to start with an 'I' or 'My' (and if speaking for the family or couple, it starts with 'We' or 'Our').
- This tool replaces nagging and threatening with respectful communication. It also works with spouses!
- For example: "I do things for children who show a positive attitude."
- Keep in mind that your 'I' Statement must not be seen as an 'empty threat'. Your child needs to know that you mean what you say and that there will be consequences if they refuse to comply.

Solutions requiring a little more time or practice:

While we have outlined examples for each tool below, it is best to refer to the full step-by-step explanation of each tool. To do so, please click on the tool title or go to the book index to find the corresponding tool.

1. Active Listening

For example: "You seem to be a bit down today and you sound a bit negative, would you like to tell me how that feels for you right now?"

2. One-on-one Time

Dedicate some regular one-to-one 'quality' time between yourself and your child.

3. Problem Solving (age 3+)

At a later time when your child is on his or her own with you, you can say something along the lines of: "When you react negatively to something that I did for you I feel really frustrated, and it doesn't encourage me to continue making efforts for you. What could we do to make sure that this doesn't happen?" And you then can do a 'Problem Solving' session with them.

Being 'bossy'

The voice of a child

My parents call me 'Miss Bossy' when actually I feel that they are way more bossy than me! All I hear from Mum and Dad is "Do this, do that". My father likes to tell me what to do by shouting it and my Mum prefers nagging. So if they don't feel I'm important enough to have a choice in what I'm allowed to do, at least I can boss around my little brother and sometimes my Mum, ('cos I know that if I go on for long enough my Mum will probably give in!). When I try to do this with my father, he gets really cross, but at least he pays attention to me and I love being able to control his tone of voice!

The voice of the All-heart parent

When my children were bossy to me I'd waver between being offended or amused depending on the situation, but I didn't stop to think what had caused their need to boss everyone about. Once I'd looked at the psychological motivations behind bossiness, I recognised that the need to tell people what to do comes from wanting more control over one's life, as well as a greater sense of 'significance'. And I also had to acknowledge that when my somewhat 'laissez-faire' instincts lead me to give in to their bossy demands, I was only reinforcing their behaviour.

The voice of the Strict parent

It is disconcerting for a parent with authoritarian tendencies to be on the receiving end of bossy behaviour from one's children. It is so easy for a battle of wills to ensue, with no real winner or change in behaviour at the end of it. But as a Strict parent, I often have to remind myself that my tendency to be bossy is what leads my children to being bossy themselves!

Quick and easy solutions: ⌛ 5 minutes max

1. Modelling
- It is natural for our children to reproduce what they see and hear.
- Be aware of this and try and reduce your own 'bossiness'!
- Try to phrase your requests in a more considerate way.
- For example: "Would you kindly pass the butter when you are ready?" Or "It would be great if you went upstairs and got ready for school."

2. Limited Choices
- This is our favourite and most effective tool to encourage cooperation. It works for most situations and ages.
- Rather than making immediate 'demands' on our children, we ask them to choose between two options (that suit *us*).
- Example: "Do you want to get up now or in five minutes?"

- This has the advantage of putting our children into 'thinking mode' rather than 'opposition mode'.
- We should use 'Limited Choices' as often as we can, because asking children to make decisions allows them to feel some control over their lives, and therefore makes them less prone to power struggles.

3. Asking Questions

- Calmly and kindly ask your child questions.
- For example: "Is this a good way to speak to your Mum?" or "Do you think I am going to want to give you what you've just asked for now that you've used this tone of voice?" or "It sounds like you want me to do something for you, can you think of a better way of asking for it?"
- You could emphasize your point by whispering, which often works to calm a situation down and encourage your child to take notice of what you say.

3. 'I' Statements

- If we focus on what we *can* control versus what we would *like* to control, we can then make a statement that we can actually enforce.
- Our 'I' Statement needs to start with an 'I' or 'My' (and if speaking for the family or couple, it starts with 'We' or 'Our').
- This tool replaces nagging and threatening with respectful communication. It also works with spouses!
- For example, say to your child gently "I listen to children who talk to me in a different tone of voice."
- Notice that this sentence is positive and not a typical: "If you don't do that, you won't be able to do that!" threat.
- Keep in mind that your 'I' Statement must not be seen as an 'empty threat'. Your child needs to know that you mean what you say and that there will be consequences if they refuse to comply.

4. Setting Rules

- Set your rule in the third person as this makes it less confrontational and increases the chances of your child respecting the rule.
- For e.g. "This is the new rule: in this house, children have to tidy their room by the end of each day."
- If your child doesn't follow the rule, you can then impose a related consequence (see below).

Solutions requiring a little more time or practice:

While we have outlined examples for each tool below, it is best to refer to the full step-by-step explanation of each tool. To do so, please click on the tool title or go to the book index to find the corresponding tool.

1. Creating Routines

With the help of your child create a routine around regular tasks, this will enables the routines to 'be the boss' and reduce power struggles.

2. Logical Consequences

Remember this is not a punishment. When your child knows that a rule or agreement exists and then chooses to break it, you can apply a Related and Reasonable consequence with empathy. For example: "It's so sad, that bossy way in which you just told me to give you that biscuit doesn't make me want to share the packet with you right now."

3. Delayed Consequences (age 4+)

When you can't apply a Logical Consequence due to circumstance, or because you feel too angry or upset, you can delay it until a later time or date. Remember, this is not a punishment because the consequence should be reasonable (and ideally related) and delivered with empathy. For example: "Sadly, because of the way you tried to order me around last night I now don't feel like going for a bike ride with you."

4. Energy Drain (age 3+)

Example: "All this bossiness is giving me an energy drain."

5. Problem Solving (age 3+)

At a later time when your child is on his or her own with you, you can say something along the lines of: "When you are this bossy to me, I don't feel like listening to you, what do you suggest would be a better solution?" And then begin a 'Problem Solving' session with your child.

'Back-talking', being rude and swearing

The voice of the Child

My parents use all kinds of words that they tell me not to use and I get totally confused by this. I often wonder why they get so wound up and sometimes angry when I swear while they often swear or speak to me rudely?! It doesn't seem fair at all! It's actually kind of fun to swear and back talk as it immediately puts my parents in a 'state', and I feel I have some control over them by just saying a few words!

The voice of the All-heart parent

When my child started back talking me I was rather dismayed! But a little research revealed that there is an 'age of rudeness', which typically happens when children hit seven years of age (although it can sometimes occur earlier). I also understood that it was crucial that I handled the situation carefully, for if I became disrespectful and angry towards her I would be merely leading her to continue talking to me in the same way. We often forget that children need to be taught why it is that manners matter so much.

The voice of the Strict parent

I cannot stand being disrespected or hearing my children swear so I tend to react very negatively and overdramatically when it happens. I needed to be reassured that it's normal for children to back talk and that it is not an indication of a permanent attitude problem. I also had to realise that labelling my children 'rude' (and telling them in pretty 'rude' terms myself how unacceptable back talking is), was not going to solve the problem!

Quick and easy solutions: ⏳ 5 minutes max

1. Modelling

- It is quite normal to let the occasional 'swearing' through without making a big deal of it. Since children have what is called 'delayed imitation' memory, it's no surprise if they end up using the same words that they hear others around them using (and they may also be unaware of the 'meaning' of the words they are using).
- We therefore need to be aware of whether our children are just copying our behaviour, and to make sure we don't use 'rude' words on them in the future.
- We also need to avoid thinking that swearing is the end of the world, and focus instead on how we react to it so that they are disinclined to do it again.
- Role playing situations where one person is rude to another and loses that person's friendship or assistance is an effective way of getting the message across.

2. 'I' Statements

- If we focus on what we can control versus what we would like to control, we can then make a statement that we can actually enforce.
- Our 'I' Statement needs to start with an 'I' or 'My' (and if speaking for the family or couple, it starts with 'We' or 'Our').
- This tool replaces nagging and threatening with respectful communication. It also works with spouses!
- Example: say to your child gently, "I give my attention to children who are polite", or "In this family we listen to people who speak to each other properly."
- Notice that this sentence is positive and not a typical: "If you don't do that, you won't be able to do that!" threat.
- Keep in mind that your 'I' Statement must not be seen as an 'empty threat'. Your child needs to know that you mean what you say and that there will be consequences if they refuse to comply.

3. 'I Feel' Messages

- Encourage your child to see his or her behaviour through your eyes. But do this with empathy rather than through blaming or shaming, otherwise the lesson will be lost.
- For example: "I feel upset that you should want to talk to your teacher/ to me in this way, how do you think it would make you feel if someone was that rude to you?"
- Encouraging your child to identify with the feelings of the 'victim' of their rudeness is a good lesson in empathy.

4. Setting Rules

- If you haven't already set a rule about swearing or back talking, now is your chance. But don't do it when you are angry because it will feel to your child like a 'telling off'!
- Set your rule in the third person as this makes it less confrontational and increases the chances of your child respecting the rule (and if you set the rule: "In this family we try very hard not to swear", it has to apply to you too!).
- Explain why swearing is 'ugly talk' and have fun exploring homemade alternatives "Oh hot muffins" or "Oh Splinglesplat!"
- If your child doesn't follow the rule, you can then impose a related consequence (see below).

Solutions requiring a little more time or practice:

While we have outlined examples for each tool below, it is best to refer to the full step-by-step explanation of each tool. To do so, please click on the tool title or go to the book index to find the corresponding tool.

1. Logical Consequences

Remember, this is not a punishment. When your child knows that a rule or agreement exists and then chooses to break it, you can apply a Related and Reasonable consequence with empathy.

2. Delayed Consequences

When you can't apply a Logical Consequence due to circumstance, or because you feel too angry or upset, you can delay it until a later time or date. Remember, this is not a punishment because the consequence should be reasonable (and ideally related) and delivered with empathy.

3. Delayed Consequences (age 4+)

When you can't apply a 'Logical Consequence' due to circumstance, or because you feel too angry or upset, you can delay it until a later time or date. Remember, this is not a punishment, so the consequence should be reasonable (and ideally related) and delivered with empathy. For example, say at a later date: "It's a shame that you still think it is ok to be rude to me, we won't worry about it now, but we will need to do something about this at a later date."

4. Energy Drain (age 3+)

Explaining that this situation is draining us of energy allows our children to realise that their actions affect others. It also allows them to understand that in order to 'repair' the situation, they should help with household tasks or give us time to replenish our energy. For e.g. "This rudeness is draining me of energy, I am going to need your help restoring my energy levels in future."

5. Problem Solving (age 3+)

At a later time, when your child is on his or her own with you, you can say something along the lines of: "When you asked me for this earlier in that rude voice, it really didn't give me any incentive to give it to you. What do you think would have been a better way to achieve what you wanted?" And then begin a 'Problem Solving' session with your child.

Lying or Fabricating

The voice of a child

When I was younger, I don't think I always knew the difference between what was real and what wasn't. So some of the time I'd tell my parents that things had happened when they had only happened in my imagination. My mother seemed to think that it was ok for me to make things up, but I remember that my father seemed to get anxious about it and lecture me about how important it is to always tell the truth. But when I was a bit older things got a bit more serious. Like the time I told my parents that I hadn't taken my sister's sweets when I had. I thought I might get away with it and I nearly did because my Mum, seeing that my Dad was about to get mad, told him that I was probably confused or something. But Dad said that it was a blatant lie and he got really mad and punished me for it. I thought to myself: "I'd better not get caught next time I do something that I shouldn't!". However, I did get caught again and so I lied again because I was so afraid of my father's reaction and his punishments.

The voice of the All-heart parent

When I was first met by a barefaced lie from one of my children, I confess to being really rather shocked! I puzzled over how someone so young and innocent would want to lie to me, particularly when I was always trying to be so understanding with them? Fortunately, I then learnt that it is totally normal for children to start lying around the age of three. Indeed, small children are capable of issuing outrageous lies with complete confidence in their own credibility! But some children lie because they have learned the pain of telling the truth. As one mother shared with us on our parenting course: "My mother taught me to lie. She reacted so badly to the truth that I decided not to tell her truths that might upset her." It is essential to teach children the importance of telling the truth, coaching them out of the habit of lying and allowing them to develop a sense of responsibility towards their own actions.

The voice of the Strict parent

I came down hard on my daughter the first time she knowingly lied to me - I felt pretty outraged and determined to stop this bad behaviour from happening again lest it lead to real delinquency. Yet I realise now that I overreacted and should have taken time to explain why it is wrong to deliberately mislead others, particularly when it leads to someone else getting into trouble. The fact is that the way we react to our children's experimentation with lies has a strong influence on whether they choose to continue lying in future. Most importantly, I should have tried to find out what had motivated the lie. Since I have worked harder at understanding what is going on in my children's minds and offered them the opportunity to 'connect' with me, the need for them to lie has dwindled away.

Quick and easy solutions: ⧖ 5 minutes max

1. Setting Rules

- Set your rule in the third person as this makes it less confrontational and increases the chances of your child respecting the rule.
- Example: "This is the new rule: in this family we value truth telling above all else."
- If your child doesn't follow the rule, you can then impose a related consequence (see below).

2. Eavesdropping

- Make sure that your child 'eavesdrops' on, or overhears, a conversation between yourself and another.
- For example: "I was so impressed to see how Maria spoke up and told the truth, even when her friend had told her to lie, it showed how grown up she was."

3. 'I Feel' Messages

- The 'I feel' messages let your child know how you feel without blaming or shaming.

- Telling our children how we feel can help them learn the importance of telling the truth.
- Example: "When you don't tell me the truth, it hurts me and makes me feel that I can't trust you."

Solutions requiring a little more time or practice:

While we have outlined examples for each tool below, it is best to refer to the full step-by-step explanation of each tool. To do so, please click on the tool title or go to the book index to find the corresponding tool.

1. Active Listening

At a later time, when everyone is relaxed, raise the subject of the 'lie' with your child and, using lots of empathy, try to understand what motivated their decision not to tell the truth. End by asking how they would act in future.

2. Logical Consequences

Remember this is not a punishment, when your child knows that a rule or agreement exists and then chooses to break it, you can apply a Related and Reasonable consequence with empathy. For example: "Unfortunately since you have lied about having done your homework, we're going to have to stay in this weekend to make sure that you do it."

3. Delayed Consequences (age 4+)

When you can't apply a 'Logical Consequence' due to circumstance, or because you feel too angry or upset, you can delay it until a later time or date. Remember, this is not a punishment so the consequence should be reasonable (and ideally related) and delivered with empathy. For example, say at a later date when your child asks you for a treat: "Sadly, because you lied to me yesterday and claimed that you hadn't taken your sister's book when you knew that you had, we won't be buying you a treat today."

4. Energy Drain (age 3+)

Example: "When I hear lies it gives me an energy drain, I'll need your help getting some energy back!"

5. Problem Solving (age 3+)

This is the most important tool for solving 'communication' issues, such as lying, because it ensures that you have a proper conversation with your child about why it is so important to tell the truth.

Once you feel calm enough to discuss the 'lie' without distress, sit down with your child and say something along the lines of: "I feel disappointed when you lie to me, because it makes it very difficult for me and others to trust you. Since telling the truth is really important ,what do you think might discourage you from telling lies in the future?"

Try and engage their listening and use solutions such as "Were you worried that if you had told me the truth you'd be upsetting me?" And then begin a 'Problem Solving' session with your child.

Wanting constant attention

The voice of a child

Sometimes I feel very alone, as if no one knows or cares if I'm there. It's really important to me to know that people care about me, particularly my parents. So I spend quite a lot of time asking for them to take notice of me, inventing reasons why I need them to be beside me all the time, answering my questions, even arguing with me. I think that my parents believe that it's enough for them to just be in the background and that I can just get on with amusing myself. I wish they could give me some proper time together to play and be friendly, rather than just being 'serious' Mum and Dad.

The voice of the All-heart parent

When one of my children seemed unusually greedy for my attention I usually gave it to them if I was able. However, I would get frustrated by the fact that the more attention I gave, the more they seemed to demand. The fact is that children naturally crave our attention, but the way they will then react to us is determined by the type of attention we have given them. I realised that I needed to avoid giving 'special service', i.e. constantly doing things for my children that they should normally be able to do themselves. Over-parenting in this way simply reinforces the attention-seeking and prevents them from building up the autonomy that will actually make them feel more 'significant'.

The voice of the Strict parent

A child constantly asking for our attention can be difficult to handle, particularly for someone like me who wants clear boundaries to be respected. My reaction was sometimes to ignore my child, hoping that she would get the message that I wasn't prepared to drop everything for her at the drop of a hat. But this wouldn't solve the problem as she would whine and start hassling me. And when I got angry because I became exasperated, I would lose the connection and she'd stop talking to me. Hardly the best outcome!

Quick and easy solutions: ⌛ 5 minutes max

1. Family Contribution

- This is one of the keys to reducing the attention-seeking as it makes our children feel more important.
- Ask your child to help you with everyday tasks as often as possible (even if you're not sure that they can do it and if it means that the task will take longer to complete!).
- For e.g. ask your child to help you with cleaning, with cooking, with carrying things, with removing leaves from garden, etc....

2. Limited Choices

- This is our favourite and most effective tool to encourage cooperation. It works for most situations and ages.
- Rather than making immediate 'demands' on our children, we ask them to choose between two options (that suit us).
- Example: "Do you want to do this now or in a couple of minutes?", "Do you want to dress up first or to do your bed first?",

"Do you want to have cereal or toast (or both?) for breakfast?", "Do you want to leave now or in five minutes?" etc.

- This has the advantage of putting our children into 'thinking mode' rather than 'opposition mode'.
- We should use 'Limited Choices' as often as we can, because asking children to make decisions allows them to feel some control over their lives, and therefore makes them less prone to power struggles.

3. 'I' Statements

- If we focus on what we can control versus what we would like to control, we can then make a statement that we can actually enforce.
- Our 'I' Statement needs to start with an 'I' or 'My' (and if speaking for the family or couple, it starts with 'We' or 'Our').
- This tool replaces nagging and threatening with respectful communication. It also works with spouses!
- For example: tell your child gently, "I help children who have already tried to do things by themselves."
- Notice that this sentence is positive and not a typical: "If you don't do that, you won't be able to do that!" threat.
- Keep in mind that your 'I' Statement must not be seen as an 'empty threat'. Your child needs to know that you mean what you say and that there will be consequences if they refuse to comply.

4. 'I Feel' Messages

- When our children whine or constantly seek our attention it helps to explain to our children what we feel.
- For example: "When you're whining and you're constantly seeking my attention, I feel frustrated because I would love to spend time with you, but I need to finish something urgently. I love you and I will spend time with you in one hour."

Solutions requiring a little more time or practice:

While we have outlined examples for each tool below, it is best to refer to the full step-by-step explanation of each tool. To do so, please click on the tool title or go to the book index to find the corresponding tool.

1. One on One Time

Dedicate some regular one-to-one 'quality' time between yourself and your child. It is a great way to encourage your child to feel more significant.

2. Creating Routines

Devise a routine (ideally with your child's help) and then stick to it, allowing routine rather than you, become the boss.

3. Problem Solving (age 3+)

At a later time, when your child is on his or her own with you, you can say something along the lines of: "When you constantly ask me for my attention I can't complete any of my tasks, what do you think would be a better way of asking for my help?" And then begin a 'Problem Solving' session with your child.

Disrespecting house rules

The voice of a child

"Do this!" "Don't do that!" "Not that way!" It's just so frustrating; there are so many things that I'm supposed to do or not do. How am I supposed to know what's right and what's wrong, or remember all the things that are asked of me? And sometimes something's ok one day but not the other, so how am I supposed to know what to do? Why do my parents always get to have things their way? Why don't I get a say in it? It's so unfair!

The voice of the All-heart parent

Research shows that rules and limits are important guidelines for children, they may initially protest them, but they will feel safer when they know that these clear and consistent boundaries exist. But putting these rules in place and making sure that they are respected and followed seemed to me to be a tricky business, because I feared sounding too authoritarian. But I soon found that setting rules for the whole family, in a spirit of respect and kindness, makes the job of parenting a great deal easier.

The voice of the Strict parent

If as a parent your expectation is that rules are to be obeyed at all times, as I once believed should be the case, you are in for a bit of a surprise! It's worth remembering that it is in younger children's natures to either forget, test, or deliberately break the rules that we set. What can seem like defiance can just be the result of a young mind struggling to take on board the way things are done and why. That said, of course it is important to make sure children follow the rules, but it's the methods we use for applying and 'enforcing' these rules that determine the quality of a family life together.

Quick and easy solutions: ⌛ 5 minutes max
1. Setting Rules

- You need to set up rules in a non-confrontational way, using the third person rather than the first, and making sure that your children know and understand why rules need to exist.
- It might be helpful to ask your children to make a list of the house rules that they can remember (in a caring kind of way) and then ask them to explain back to you why they think the rules are there.
- For children aged four and up, you can try to work out some new rules together, for example during a Family Meeting (see corresponding tool).
- Remember it is perfectly legitimate for a rule to be there because Mummy or Daddy needs it to be as long as it is delivered with empathy.

- If your child doesn't follow the rule, you can then impose a related consequence (see below).
- Try to limit rules to what is really unacceptable so that they don't become too many and too daunting.

2. 'I' Statements

- Being aware of what you can control versus what you would like to control, then make a non-negotiable statement that you can actually enforce.
- It needs to start with 'I' or 'my' (and if speaking for the family or couple, it starts with 'we' or 'our').
- "I give dessert to children who have stayed seated at the table and finished their meal", or "I listen to children who respect our family rules."

3. 'I Feel' Messages

- Try to let your child know how you feel without blaming or shaming.
- For e.g. Tell your child "It upsets me when you break our family rules, I wonder how you would feel if I broke *your* rules?"
- Your child will begin to appreciate that his or her behaviour has an effect on others, which in turn has an effect on him or her.

Solutions requiring a little more time or practice:

While we have outlined examples for each tool below, it is best to refer to the full step-by-step explanation of each tool. To do so, please click on the tool title or go to the book index to find the corresponding tool.

1. Logical Consequences

Remember, this is not a punishment. When your child knows that a rule or agreement exists and then chooses to break it, you can apply a Respectful, Reasonable and Related consequence with empathy. For example: "What a shame, as you know our rule is that we remain seated for our meals, and since you left the table to go play, dinner is now over for you."

2. Delayed Consequences (age 4+)

When you can't apply a 'Logical Consequence' due to circumstance, or because you feel too angry or upset, you can delay it until a later time or date. Remember, this is not a punishment, so the consequence should be reasonable (and ideally related) and delivered with respect and empathy. For example, say at a later date: "It's a shame, since you broke the rule about fighting in the car I'm now not going to be able to take you on that trip to the ice cream parlour."

3. Problem Solving (age 3+)

At a later time, when your child is on his or her own with you, you can say something along the lines of: "You seem to have difficulty following the house rules, what do you suggest we do to make sure that you don't break them again in the future?" And then begin a 'Problem Solving' session with your child.

Feeling insecure or lacking confidence

The voice of a child

Other people seem to feel fine about themselves, but often I don't feel very good being me. Sometimes Mum and Dad get annoyed at me for not being able to know what to do for myself, but most of the time they are fine doing it for me. From the way they act, I think I need protecting because I'm not as strong or as smart as other children.

The voice of the All-heart parent

I have quite over-protective tendencies and therefore when I see my child distressed or feeling insecure, my immediate reaction is to try and make everything better for them. Unfortunately, after a while I began to notice that too much running in to 'save' my child was leading them to become dependent on me to trouble-shoot any situation that might be tricky for them. I discovered that it is far better to empower them by giving them the tools to help themselves. I also began to allow them to train their 'disappointment' muscle by learning through their own 'affordable' mistakes.

The voice of the Strict parent

I am quite impatient; this can lead me to inadvertently overlook my children's feelings of insecurity over something, which can make me appear intolerant or uncaring to them. Unfortunately, my frustration just serves to worsen their feelings of not being 'good enough'. Part of my parenting journey involved learning that insecurity is a feeling that needs to be handled with care. Once I started using empathy and gaining more insight into my child's perception of the world, I was able to encourage my children to have a good sense of self. Avoid the temptation to label a child as 'insecure', boxing children in this way is never helpful to either parent or child.

Quick and easy solutions: ⏳ 5 minutes max
1. Empathy and Validation
- Acknowledge your child's feelings about their situation with an empathic statement.
- For example: "I can tell you are really upset about something."
- Do not tell them "It probably isn't as bad as you think."
- Do ask "Is there something that would help the situation?"

2. Limited Choices
- When children are given choices, they move from 'opposition mode' into 'thinking mode', and become interested in listening rather than arguing.
- A child who feels insecure probably feels disempowered. So what better way to make them feel confident and in control than by asking them to make as many choices as possible?
- These choices should be limited to two options, both of which are agreeable to you.

- For example, you can ask your child: "Would you like to ask your friend for a play-date at drop off or pick up time?"

3. Positive Redirection

- Try and limit the amount of times that you use the word 'No' and replace it with more positive sentences.
- For example, instead of telling your child, "NO we can't go to ... because you had bad marks and you need to do more homework", try instead "YES we can go there as soon as you've finished your homework."

Solutions requiring a little more time or practice:

While we have outlined examples for each tool below, it is best to refer to the full step-by-step explanation of each tool. To do so, please click on the tool title or go to the book index to find the corresponding tool.

1. Acknowledgement and Encouragement

Try to encourage and praise them on what they are doing well by using descriptive praise. But avoid over-praising, lest they begin to start discounting the authenticity or quality of your appreciation. When your child has achieved something, ask them what part of their work they feel particularly proud of, and then reflect it back to them. For example, if they have made something special ask: "How do you think your clay cat looks?" and then "I'm hearing that you feel really proud of getting it to stand up and I agree, you've obviously put a lot of effort and thought into making it."

2. Active Listening

In order to get an insight into your child's thinking so that you are able to help them 'let go' of their negativity, let them express their negative feelings without judgement. Avoid supressing their feelings by immediately suggesting your own solutions.

<u>3. Generating Solutions (age 4+)</u>

Once you have used Active Listening, you can ask your child: "What could you do that would make you feel better about it? Do you want to know what other children like to do in your situation?"

Taking too long to do everything

The voice of a child

When you are little, everyone expects you to know how much time has passed when you aren't even able to tell the time! Most mornings I sort of lose track of things and can't quite remember what I am supposed to be doing next. My Mum thought that it meant that she had to do everything for me, so now I just wait for her to tell me what I need to do. But my Dad gets cross and tells her that I'm spoilt and that I'm getting unable to do things for myself. The two of them tend to end up arguing about me in front of me, which isn't very nice for me I can tell you!

The voice of the All-heart parent

Most children, particularly in the early years, often have a very flexible attitude to time, at one moment they need to do something absolutely NOW while at others, the same task will take them an age. This unpredictability would leave me very confused as to how to react to, or 'police' their preparations, or lack of. Often I'd feel like I had given in too early, but under time pressure, I mistakenly believed that I had no alternative but to do things for them.

The voice of the Strict parent

I used to think that a father's job was to tell his children what to do and when to do it and that his children should follow his lead. It took me a while to realise the difference between 'ordering' and coaching our children. But gradually I began to understand that while my children needed to understand that there are necessary time constraints, I was actually encouraging them to become over-dependant on me, telling them what to do was not at all helpful to either my children or myself in the long run!

Quick and easy solutions: ⧖ 5 minutes max
1. Planning Ahead
- If your child tends to take too long to do things in the morning, you can decide to wake him or her up 15 minutes earlier. Parents often tell us that this alone can make a huge difference in reducing the morning stress!
- There are also a few things that you can prepare in advance, for example, give them Limited Choices (see below) of what they would like to wear the next day the night before. You can also give them a choice of what they would like for breakfast, etc....

2. Limited Choices
- This is our favourite and most effective tool to encourage cooperation. It works for most situations and ages.
- Rather than making immediate 'demands' on our children, we ask them to choose between two options (that suit *us*).
- For example: "Would you like to make your bed first, or would you rather brush your hair?" or "Would you rather use the 30 minutes that you have until breakfast to get dressed, or use just ten minutes for dressing and use the remaining 20 minutes to play a fun game with me?"
- This has the advantage of putting our children into 'thinking mode' rather than 'opposition mode'.
- We should use 'Limited Choices' as often as we can, because asking children to make decisions allows them to feel some control over their lives, and therefore makes them less prone to power struggles.

3. 'I' Statements

- If we focus on what we *can* control versus what we would *like* to control, we can then make a statement that we can actually enforce.
- Our 'I' Statement needs to start with an 'I' or 'My' (and if speaking for the family or couple, it starts with 'We' or 'Our').
- This tool replaces nagging and threatening with respectful communication. It also works with spouses!
- For example: gently say to your child, "My car leaves in five minutes and I take children to school dressed or not dressed."
- Notice that this sentence is positive and not a typical: "If you don't do that, you won't be able to do that!" threat.

4. Setting Rules

- Set your rule in the third person as this makes it less confrontational, and increases the chances of your child respecting the rule.
- For e.g. "This is the new rule: in this house, children have to get dressed before breakfast."
- If your child doesn't follow the rule, you can then impose a related consequence (see below).

Solutions requiring a little more time or practice:

While we have outlined examples for each tool below, it is best to refer to the full step-by-step explanation of each tool. To do so, please click on the tool title or go to the book index to find the corresponding tool.

1. Logical Consequences

Remember, this is not a punishment. When your child knows that a rule or agreement exists and then chooses to break it, you can apply a Related and Reasonable consequence with empathy. For example: "It's such a shame, as you've taken so long to get dressed, we're not going to be able to go to the park this morning".

2. Problem Solving (age 3+)

At a later time, when your child is on their own with you, you can say something along the lines of: "I feel frustrated when you won't get ready in time because it makes us late for work and school. What could we do next time to help you get ready faster? Do you want ideas of what other children have tried?"_And then begin a 'Problem Solving' session with your child.

3. Creating Routines

Work out a routine with your child that describes, and even illustrates, each activity beforehand. A step-by-step 'schedule' acts as a useful reference point and aide memoire.

Hooked on Screens, TV, iPads and other game tablets

The voice of a child

My parents are always nagging me to get off the iPad or to turn off the TV. But I love my games and programmes. What's wrong with that? My Mum and Dad are always on their tablets and phones, tex-ting, tweeting, playing games or 'just checking'. I don't understand their reactions at all. One minute they are putting a screen into my hand so that they can 'have the chance to get on with something', and the next minute they are grabbing the screen from me and shouting that I watch far too much and that it rots my brain.

The voice of the All Heart parent

Most parents get a shock when they discover the 'magnetic' affect that screens have on children. Once children discover the power of the moving image, they are often hooked. Unfortunately, re-search shows that considerable TV viewing and other screens can have significant negative effects on children , so I had to force myself to set clear rules and to teach my children that screen time is a privi-lege - unless it is used for homework - and that privileges come with responsibilities. They now accept the rules that we have set as a family, but of course, they try to negotiate some additional time. What I have found is that if I suggest to do something together, whether be it cooking, playing a board game, dressing up or anything else, it will take precedence over screens; time with us can be more precious to our children (until their teenage years), particularly when they get used to this from an early age.

The voice of the Strict parent

I used to get angry when my children wouldn't stop playing with the tablet or phone when I asked them to. But I soon realised that I was wasn't being entirely fair, since I was often prone to picking up my own phone or tablet mid conversation or mid-meal 'just to check' or to answer a call. I realised that when I don't touch my phone in their company, they are much less likely to ask for it. Screen time is a modern phenomenon, which we are all learning to navigate, but our household has learned that the best defence against erratic or widespread use is to set very clear rules and boundaries around when and where we can use them.

Quick and easy solutions: ⌛ 5 minutes max
1. Limited Choices
- When children are given choices they move from 'opposition mode' into 'thinking mode', and become interested in listening rather than arguing.
- Rather than making immediate 'demands' on our children, we allow them to feel some con-trol over their lives by asking them to choose between two options (that suit us).
- Example: "Do you want to play with the iPad for 30 minutes now or after you have finished your homework," or "Would you rather we look at old photos and do a collage of the last year or make cookies with me?"

- This has the advantage of putting our children in to 'thinking mode' rather than 'opposition mode'.
- We should use 'Limited Choices' as often as we can, because asking children to make decisions makes them feel more respected and receptive, and less prone to power struggles.

2. Setting Rules

- Set your rule in the third person as this makes it less confrontational and increases the chanc-es of your child respecting the rule.
- For example: "Children who want to use the iPad/play an electronic game need to have fin-ished their homework," or "The rule in this house is that children can spend 30 minutes on screens every day - you can choose between TV and iPad."
- One suggestion is to create 'vouchers' with a certain amount of time printed on them (e.g. 60 minutes of the iPad) that are then distributed fairly amongst your children on a weekly basis. The understanding is that once the children have 'spent' their vouchers, they are not allowed to have any more screen time for the rest of the week. This system encourages children to be responsible for using their 'allocated' time wisely. And it also helps them realise that once they have used up their vouchers they will need to find other things to entertain themselves.
- The American Academy of Pediatrics recommends that parents establish 'screen-free' zones at home by making sure there are no televisions, computers or video games in children's bed-rooms . We realise that this is not easy to enforce, particularly if children need some form of screen to do their homework.
- If your child doesn't follow the rules, you can then impose a related consequence (see below).

Solutions requiring a little more time or practice:

While we have outlined examples for each tool below, it is best to refer to the full step-by-step expla-nation of each tool. To do so, please click on the tool title or go to the book index to find the corre-sponding tool.

1. Playing

When your child asks you to spend time on a screen, try and suggest an alternative activity they can do and, time permitting, join them. It can be anything from a board game, cooking together, planning a fancy dress party for the next weekend, investigating the local area, taking notes and photographs and planning activities to do for the family, etc.

2. Modelling

Realising that what you do can greatly influence your children, make sure that you can restrict your own screen time in front of them for example, by not keeping the TV on for long periods of time (and particularly at dinner time). Also make sure that there are lots of real activities to compete with elec-tronic entertainment.

3. Diffusing Whining and Arguing (3+)

If your child is requesting a screen and you have explained that it is not the right time, you can then respond to their whining or arguing by repeating an 'empathetic statement' like "I know", or "I heard you", or "I love you too much to argue". - Say this as often as needed and without giving in, getting angry or raising your voice.

4. Logical Consequences

Remember this is not a punishment, when your child knows that a rule or agreement exists and then chooses to break it, you can apply a Related and Reasonable consequence with empathy. For exam-ple: "Sadly since you chose to break the rule about agreeing to leave the screen when asked, I am now going to have to take it away for a couple of days." This is a totally related and respectful consequence and it is important that you stick to it to make sure your children respect the rules that you have set.

5. Delayed Consequences (4 +)

'When you can't apply a logical consequence due to circumstance, or because you feel too angry or upset, you can delay this consequence until a later time or date. Remember this is not a punishment, the consequence should be reasonable and related and delivered with empathy. For example: "Since you refused to get off the screen when we were at Grandad's, you're not going to be able to play any electronic game today."

6. Energy Drain (3+)

For example: "When you chose to watch a series on my iPad without asking permission, this gave me an energy drain, and I'm going to have to do something about it but not now." And when your child asks you to do something with them a few days later, you can say "You remember how I got that en-ergy drain the other day? Well, I still don't have enough energy to do this with you today, try me an-other time".

7. Problem Solving (3+)

At a later time when your child is on his or her own with you, you can say something along the lines of: "When you appear to ignore my requests to stop using the iPad, I feel disrespected and upset. You seem to be having trouble staying away from the screens?" And then begin a 'Problem Solving' session with your child, bringing ideas of other real activities that she could do or you could do together, (see above in Playing) and most importantly, remember to ask them how they would like to be reminded when their screen time is over.

Your notes

Your notes

Endnotes

1. Bronson, Po and Merryman, Ashley, *Nurture Shock*, Ebury Press, 2009
2. Siegel, Daniel, *Parenting From the Inside Out*, Jeremy P. Tarcher, 2003
3. Baumrind, Diana, Effects of Authoritative Parental Control on Child Behavior, Child Development, 1966
4. Baumrind, Diana, *Childcare practices anteceding three patterns of preschool behaviour*, Genetic Psychology Monographs, 1967
5. Baumrind, Diana, *Childcare practices anteceding three patterns of preschool behaviour*
6. Baumrind, Diana, *Effects of Authoritative Parental Control on Child Behavior*
7. Coopersmith, Stanley, *The antecedents of self-esteem*, Consulting Psychologists Press, 1967
8. Dreikurs, Rudolf, *Children: The Challenge*, First Plume Printing, 1990
9. Dreikurs, Rudolf, *Children: The Challenge*
10. Dreikurs, Rudolf, *Children: The Challenge*
11. Siegel, Daniel, *Parenting From the Inside Out*
12. Fay, Charles, *Love and Logic newsletter*, January, 29, 2014
13. Webster-Stratton, *The Incredible Years*, Incredible Years, 2005, p70
14. Newberg, Andrew, and Waldman, Mark Robert, *The neuroscience of communication*, 2012
15. Tool adapted from *Parenting with Love and Logic*, Navpress, 2006
16. Siegel, Daniel, *Parenting From the Inside Out*
17. Shefali Tsabary, *The Conscious Parent: Transforming Ourselves, Empowering Our Children*, Namaste Publishing, 2010
18. Shefali Tsabary, *The Conscious Parent*
19. Hawn, Goldie, *10 Mindful minutes*, Piatkus, 2011
20. Hawn, Goldie, *10 Mindful minutes*

21. Kenneth, R. Ginsburg, *The Importance of Play in Promoting Healthy Child Development and Maintaining Strong Parent-Child Bonds*, American Academy of Pediatrics, Vol. 119 No. 1 January 1, 2007

22. Biddulph, Steve, *Raising Boys,* Harper Thorsons, 2010

23. Hawn, Goldie, *10 Mindful minutes*

24. Siegel, Daniel, *Parenting From the Inside Out*

25. Siegel, Daniel, *Parenting From the Inside Out*

26. Medina, John, *Brain Rules,* Pear Press, 2014

27. Gottman, John, *Raising an Emotionally Intelligent Child*, Simon and Chuster, 1997

28. Gottman, John, *Raising an Emotionally Intelligent Child*

29. Dweck, Carol, *Mindset: The New Psychology of Success*, Ballantine Books, 2007

30. Rosenberg, Marshall, *Nonviolent Communication: a Language of Life*, Puddle Dancer Press, 2003

31. Markham, Laura, *Peaceful Parent, Happy Kids*, Penguin Books, 2012

32. Nelsen, Jane, *Positive Discipline*, Ballantine Books, 2013

33. Siegel, Daniel, *Parenting From the Inside Out*

34. MacKenzie, Michael J. and Nicklas, Eric and Waldfogel, Jane and Brooks-Gunn, Jeanne, *Spanking and Child Development Across the First Decade of Life,* 2013

35. Markham, Laura, Aha Parenting, URL: http://www.ahaparenting.com/parenting-tools/positive-discipline/Consequences_Punishment

36. Tool adapted from *Love and Logic Magic for Early Childhood*, Love and Logic, 2000 and *Positive Discipline*, Ballantine Books, 2013

37. Tool adapted from *Love and Logic Magic for Early Childhood*

38. Cline, Foster, *Love and Logic newsletter*, April, 2, 2014

39. Nelsen, Jane, *Positive Discipline blog*, http://blog.positivediscipline.com/2012/10/show-faith.html#sthash.lCo2GvJr.dpuf

40. Rossmann, Marty, *Involving children in household tasks: is it worth the effort?*, University of Minnesota, 2002

41. Fabes, Richard A.; Fultz, Jim; Eisenberg, Nancy; May-Plumlee, Traci; Christopher, F. Scott

    Effects of rewards on children's prosocial motivation: A socialization study, 1989, AND Warneken and Tomasello, *Extrinsic rewards undermine altruistic tendencies in 20-month-olds*, 2008

42. Tool adapted from *Positive Discipline*

43. Reivich, Karen, Shatte, Andrew, The Resilience Factor, Three Rivers Press, 2002

44. Ginott, Haim, *Between Parent and Child*, Crown Publications, 2004

45. Gottman, John, *Raising an Emotionally Intelligent Child*, Simon and Chuster, 1997

46. Mischel, Walter, *The Marshmallow Test: Mastering Self-control*, Little Brown and Company, 2014

47. Mischel, Walter, *The Marshmallow Test: Mastering Self-control*

48. Sigman, Aric, *Visual voodoo: the biological impact of watching TV*, The Biologist, Volume 54, 2007

49. American Academy of Pediatrics, *http://www.aap.org/en-us/advocacy-and-policy/aap-health-initiatives/Pages/Media-and-Children.aspx*

Further Reading and Sources

Aldort, Naomi, *Raising our Children, Raising Ourselves*, Book Publishers Network, 2005

Bronson, Po and Merryman, Ashley, *Nurture Shock*, Ebury Press, 2009

Biddulph, Steve, Raising Boys, Harper Thorsons, 2010

Carey, Tanith, *Taming The Tiger Parent, Robinson*, 2014

Dreikurs, Rudolf, *Children: The Challenge*, First Plume Printing, 1990

Dweck, Carol, *Mindset: The New Psychology of Success*, Ballantine Books, 2007

Faber, Adele and Mazlish, Elaine, *How to Talk so Kids Will Listen and Listen so Kids Will Talk*, Avon Books, 1999

Faber, Adele and Mazlish, Elaine, *Siblings Without Rivalry*, Piccadilly Press, 1999

Fay, Jim and Cline, Foster, *Parenting with Love and Logic*, Navpress, 2006

Fay, Jim and Charles, *Love and Logic Magic for Early Childhood*, Love and Logic, 2000

Gordon, Thomas, *Parent Effectiveness Training*, Three River Press, 2000

Goleman, Daniel, *Emotional Intelligence: Why it Can Matter More Than IQ*, Bloomsbury, 1996

Gottman, John, *Raising an Emotionally Intelligent Child*, Simon and Chuster, 1997

Ginott, Haim, *Between Parent and Child*, Crown Publications, 2004

Hawn, Goldie, *10 Mindful minutes*, Piatkus, 2011

James, Oliver, *They F*** You Up: How to Survive Family Life*, Bloomsbury, 2006

James, Oliver, *How not to f*** them up*, Vermillion, 2011

Kohn, Alfie, *Unconditional Parenting*, Atria Books, 2005

Kohn, Alfie, *Punished by Rewards*, Houghton Mifflin, 2000

Markham, Laura, *Peaceful Parent, Happy Kids*, Penguin Books, 2012

Medina, John, *Brain Rules - 12 principles for surviving and thriving at work, home and school*, Pear Press, 2014

Mischel, Walter, *The Marshmallow Test: Mastering Self-control*, Little Brown and Company, 2014

Nelsen, Jane, *Positive Discipline*, Ballantine Books, 2013

Nelsen, Jane and Lott, Lynn, and Glen, Stephen, *A-Z*, Three Rivers Press, 2007

Mc Cready, Amy, *If I Have To Tell You One More Time*, Penguin, 2012

Palmer, Sue, *Toxic Childhood*, Orion Books, 2007

Palmer, Sue, *Detoxing Childhood*, Orion Books, 2008

Reivich, Karen and Shatte, Andrew, *The Resilience Factor*, Three Rivers Press, 2002

Sanders, Matthew, *Every Parent*, Penguin Books, 2004

Shefali Tsabary, *The Conscious Parent: Transforming Ourselves, Empowering Our Children*, Namaste Publishing, 2010

Siegel, Daniel, *Parenting From the Inside Out*, Jeremy P. Tarcher, 2003

Siegel, Daniel, *The Whole Brain Child*, Bantam, 2012

Stoll Lillard, Angeline, *Montessori - The science behind the genius*, Oxford University Press, 2007

Webster-Stratton, *The Incredible Years*, Incredible Years, 2005

Acknowledgements

We would like to give credit to all the inspiring people who've dedicated their lives to improving parenting and child development all over the world, and without whom creating our content and tools would not have been possible, such as: Jane Nelsen of Positive Discipline, Jim and Charles Fay of Love and Logic, Alfie Kohn, Daniel Siegel, John Gottman, Haim Ginott, Adele Faber and Elaine Mazlish, Rudolf Dreikurs, Alfred Adler, Maria Montessori and many more!

We would like to thank our co-writer Katie Sampson. Her input and her dedication have been invaluable in adapting all the material from our parenting courses and our research to write this book.

We want to also thank our editor, Jacq Burns. Her expert feedback and her midas touch have been instrumental in getting this book through to the finish line.

Thank you also to Christopher Lascelles from Crux Publishing (www.cruxpublishing.com) for his valuable advice.

Last but not least, thank you to all the experts and friends who have spent time reading the drafts of our manuscript to give us very useful feedback. Just to name a few who's feedback has been very valuable, Sue Palmer – Author of Toxic Childhood, Grendon Haines - School Psychologist at Harrow, Stephen Adams-Langley - Senior Clinical Consultant at Place2be.org.uk, Tanith Carey – award winning author and journalist, Cristina Holst, Elaine Chestney, Elena Tricca, Sarah Cameron and Patrice Gorin.

Index

About the Authors

Carole is a Montessori trained teacher, a systems relationship coach and an NLP practitioner. She is passionate about helping parents on their parenting journey and has more than 14 years of experience teaching young children and working with parents to help them improve their relationship with their kids.

Nadim holds an MBA from INSEAD. He is a systems relationship coach and a serial entrepreneur. He has expanded companies in three continents in such diverse sectors as retail, telecoms, home management and car finance. He is passionate about sharing the transformative parenting tools that have made such a difference in his family life.

As parents of three children, Carole and Nadim wanted to make their family life more harmonious and enjoyable despite their different parenting styles. So life-changing were their discoveries that they have devoted their lives to turning what they learnt into highly effective parenting tools to share, support and guide other parents on their parenting journey. They founded the Best of Parenting company to offer services tailored to parents' individual needs including parenting courses, private coaching sessions, a trouble-shooting App and the highly acclaimed website www.bestofparenting.com.